BONUS GIFTS FROM DAVID ROY NEWBY

As my way of saying thanks for buying this book, I'm pleased to give you 4 bonuses worth over $821.00. But there's a small catch. All I ask is that you tell your friends about my book and invite them to invest in it, too. My wife and sons appreciate it.

Here's the 4 FREE Bonuses You'll Receive:

1. ***"Beyond Billions" BONUS Chapter.*** Learn how to model King Solomon's process for picking joint venture partners that made him a trillionaire worth as much as the richest 400 Americans combined. ($19.95 value)

2. **Family Vault Meeting planner.** Use this to plan and experience powerful annual retreats with your family in a simple, easy to learn format. ($297 value)

3. ***Solomon Says*** **app beta tester access.** This app is like having your favorite 10 billionaires on speed dial to ask questions when you need the best answer... only better as Solomon was the best business person ever. ($4.95 value)

4. **LegacyBuilders Consultation Credit.** Once you read this book, if you're one of the 5 percent

of people who actually use your new knowledge to improve your life, you'll want to take the next step. This entitles you to a $500 credit towards a LegacyBuilders consultation, where we'll help you build your BEST legacy possible. ($500+ value)

To claim your bonuses, NOW go to this site:
http://www.BeyondBillions.com/Bonuses.html

WHAT READERS ARE SAYING...

"David Roy Newby's techniques will enable you to build a strong legacy for your family... and find and fix the cracks that likely exist in your current legacy/estate plan."

David Green,
Founder and CEO, Hobby Lobby

"Men, especially as heads of family, as business owners, are alone on a lonely journey of identity and creators of extreme wealth. Every single owner, head of family office, estate planner, and advisor to the wealthy needs to read 'Beyond Billions'!"

Robin Coady Smith,
Succession Planner to Billionaires, PrCio.com

"David Roy Newby's 'Beyond Billions' is beyond inspirational. It's transformative, and in all the right ways. Having come from a fatherless home myself, his personal stories resonate well with me. He touches on ancient, fundamental elements of wealth creation and preservation that are ignored by the vast majority of estate planners today. Don't delay. Read 'Beyond Billions' and take action today. No matter your endeavors, I promise you: it will greatly benefit you, & everyone who knows you."

Alexander Doak,
Philippines entrepreneur

"'Beyond Billions' is a provocative, paradigm-challenging look at the all too common frustration and failure by hard-charging, high-achieving entrepreneurs and top executives with regard to family influence, transferring wisdom, not just wealth. In a complete consideration of what you are doing and why you are doing it, this has a place. Making, taking, and accumulating is all fine. I am Ayn Rand-ian about enlightened self-interest and earned privilege. But there is also something, as David puts it, beyond millions or billions, beyond scorekeeping. Tapping King Solomon as inspiration, he has done an interesting job of raising both philosophical and practical questions."

Dan Kennedy, consultant to multi-billion dollar companies & author; www.DanKennedy.com

"The principles discussed in this book give us a solid strategy for creating a lasting legacy that will impact lives for generations to come. Being a father to 7 children, we started a family foundation in 2008 with the goal of teaching our kids while simultaneously giving them opportunities to apply what they've learned. I'm always looking for resources that will aid us in communicating with and teaching our children so we can continue building our family legacy. 'Beyond Billions' is a great resource!"

Kevin Thompson, co-founder, Relationship Accelerator Network

"This book is a MUST READ for anyone looking to secure their family's financial (and even spiritual) legacy. In 'Beyond Billions,' David Roy Newby lays out a clear, easy to follow plan for creating a lasting legacy of multigenerational wealth and shared values within your family. David's unique concept of holding annual "Family Vault Meetings" is something I've never heard anyone else talk about, and I personally plan on doing one with my own children soon. Most wealthy people only look at estate planning from a tax & financial perspective. However, armed with this groundbreaking book, you will be able to secure and ensure your family's TRUE legacy for generations to come."

Eric Graham,
Marketing consultant to multiple
$100M+ companies & founder
of ConversionDoctor.com

"I am so grateful that David took the time to figure this all out. You can tell that David has done his homework on this important topic and the research he shares astounds me! I want to do better with my legacy and this book will be a great resource. I've seen families crumble because of a poorly planned transitions or spoil the next generation with too much money and too little responsibility. This book lays out a clear and easy to follow system to make sure your legacy thrives long after you've moved on. Thank you for this gift David, the legacy you are creating is massive!"

David Boufford, creator of Good News Network

"I've spent countless hours over the years in the personal space of some of the wealthiest families in America. I learned simply by observing them that children of successful parents can suffer self-destruction fueled by various dysfunctions born of a rich upbringing devoid of appreciation for what the last generation accomplished for the next's benefit. It takes work, foresight, communication, and planning in order to avoid the pitfalls mentioned above. 'Beyond Billions' highlights how those areas can be addressed and navigated in order to nurture the most desirable outcomes of generational wealth and happiness."

Joey Atlas, creator of SculptAFit Home Gym

"As a marketing consultant having turned huge companies around, I'm impressed. David Roy Newby teaches you principles that enable you to not only have money, but grow the money you have and to transfer the skillsets to your children. Is that important? It's one of the most vital things you can do. This book is essential not only to read but to implement."

**Joel Bauer, best-selling author
and master perceptionist,
www.PersuasionFoundation.com**

BEYOND BILLIONS

Create Lasting Wealth
Using Trillionaire
Solomon's Success Secrets

David Roy Newby

Foreword by Tim Wessel

Dearborn, MI

Published by Straight Arrow Press
3319 Greenfield Rd #369, Dearborn MI 48120, USA

Beyond Billions
David Roy Newby

www.BeyondBillions.com

ISBN: 978-0-692-06160-2

Hardcover Edition

DEDICATION

I dedicate this book to my two dads who taught me to have fun and be loyal, and to my wife and sons Benjamin and Simon, who have inspired me to be a better father, a better husband, and a better leader- to be the man I was created to be.

And to my Mom Violet, who taught me to ask questions and seek wisdom with my whole heart.

Maraming salamat!
("Thank You" in Filipino)

CONTENTS

FOREWORD

by Tim Wessel

D avid Newby is one of the most unique individuals I have ever known. Meet him in person and I think you'll agree. His colorful and unique outlooks, specifically his "out of the box" ways of thinking and viewing problems and opportunities are different. Different in a God-given, thought provoking way you'll find in these pages.

I'm sure many readers will purchase this book wishing to further fulfill their financial desires. For sure, they will find valuable information about money, financial instruments, wealth preservation, and creating a long-lasting legacy. Featuring the real-life stories of several billionaires (many of which David interviewed for this book) and the most successful businessperson of all time, you should have full confidence that the wisdom in this book has been tested over many generations.

From my perspective, *Beyond Billions* is also a book about the redemptive insights of a reborn man.

I have known David Newby since... well, since before I had any grey hair. For twelve years, I was a Celebrate Recovery pastor at the Brighton Nazarene Church in southeast Michigan. I remember the day I met David well. His enthusiasm and desire to listen and share was positively contagious— all attributes a pastor desires and needs from his parishioners.

I soon learned that beneath the smile and warm handshake was a broken man, who much like me, was abused as a child and as a youth suffered amidst a dark cloud of sin that had pervaded his family for generations. Yet, as he was wonderfully knit in his mother's womb, God had wonderful incredible plans in store for David. Plans that included a true rags-to-riches story, then back to rags as pride led to setbacks in his life, to a new beginning now with that hard-gained wisdom.

I hope reading these pages encourages you to create your own unique vision for yourself and your family. Proverbs 13:22 states, "A good person leaves an inheritance for their children's children." David's useable application of having frequent Family Vault Meetings (FVM) is profound and 100% applicable for parents and grandparents at every financial vantage point. David's understanding of appreciating each child's unique value and contribution regardless of career path or occupation underscores the pivotal role parents play in building a strong foundation for raising healthy and confident children, and a lasting legacy. It's awesome. He has poured his heart and soul into this project like few authors can.

I can personally attest to the power of intentionally transforming your family's legacy. My wife and I came from a place of brokenness and dysfunction, and we chose to do it differently than what we had experienced. We started from scratch and learned wisdom from experts, our peers, and mentors who could help guide us to the best ways to raise our children.

From all this great input, we live by a family creed, rally cries, intentional family time, and empowerment of our children through daily practices and annual Family Vault Meetings.

We are blessed to be enjoying great fruits from these intentional family legacy building efforts, and in *Beyond Billions*, David will be sharing several of the tools my family uses as well as many others. We have been teaching other families how to get these same benefits for years, and we look forward to working with David to help families improve their lives and see every family enjoy a powerful legacy.

With the right set of eyes, we can see ourselves in the biographical narratives of others. We are all sinners and saints alike. Here, David invites us in and openly shares how experiencing the healing power of forgiveness and learning from major mistakes dramatically improved his life, and how you can learn from both the victories and mistakes of some of the most successful people of all time as well. You can take a page or two from this book and learn how a fresh perspective can change your family's path for the better, too.

With a renewed and open mind, I hope and pray that you may live an abundant life, rich in all areas, and that your reading of *Beyond Billions* will be richly rewarded with a radically improved long-lasting legacy for you, your work, and your family.

Tim Wessel
Thrive Head Coach
www.ThriveCoaching.net

INTRODUCTION

Why You Want This Book

Y ou want to leave the most powerful legacy possible for your family, your business, and the worthy causes you passionately support, right? You want to make sure those you care about are equipped to carry on your success, correct? And you want to make sure what you leave behind isn't squandered, yes?

> **You want to make sure those you care about are equipped to carry on your success, yes?**

If so, then you're at the right place, friend; this book will help you accomplish all of those objectives, and I congratulate you on making a wise investment of your time reading this to help make those desires your reality.

The high percentage of wealthy families that fall apart when the parent(s) that created the wealth dies is simply staggering. Despite the best plans made by pricy advisors, 90% of estate plans fail. Despite the parents' best efforts to prepare their children, usually a family business doesn't last much longer than 1-2 generations after the founder steps down and is no longer running it.[1]

I don't know about you, but traditional estate planning techniques failing 90% of the time really disappoints me... and it makes me mad too. *With all the hard work, investments of time and money, and planning you've done to make a better life for your family and those you care about, you should at LEAST*

The high % of wealthy families that fall apart when the founder dies- 90%- is simply staggering.

have a better than 50/50 chance for those you leave behind to succeed once you're gone, right? **As you likely know already, to succeed you have to accurately deal with what *is*,** not what you wish was the case. In reality, *you're headed for a less than 10% success rate long-term if you follow traditional advice.*

The reality is, you're headed for a less than 10% success rate long-term if you follow traditional advice.

To avoid this fate for YOUR family, it's vital that you intentionally choose the legacy you want to leave behind, then implement your plan to do so. This book will help you do just that!

As a successful executive and entrepreneur, you also know that almost all decisions are made first emotionally and then backed up with logic. As such, I'm going to lay out for you the two most likely scenarios that your family and your business will go through in the following years depending on what actions you take regarding your legacy starting today. Please imagine these two scenarios in as much detail possible in your mind, so that your emotions will be engaged and you'll be inspired to decide once and for all that you will NOT leave your family with a 90% chance of failing. Let's begin.

LEGACY SCENARIO #1 – This is the legacy you can begin building today by implementing the process outlined in this book:

When you do what only 10% of your successful peers know how to and are willing to do to create a positive, powerful, lasting legacy, here are the results you'll likely experience: your family works in harmony, your children feel like they're a valuable part of the family, and old wounds are healed.

You can NOW create a new legacy using this book.

Your family works towards common goals, and your heirs are prepared to either take over your business when you're gone or to ensure your business keeps serving your customers long-term. Your heirs are empowered to know how to manage your estate well while you're still alive, giving you the satisfaction of knowing that whenever you are unable to or unwilling to run your business and manage your affairs, everything's in good hands to carry on profitably.

The charities you support make a BIG impact on those they support/empower, and you have peace of mind knowing that every charity dollar you give earns the maximum return ("social ROI") possible, avoiding waste. Your business runs

Imagine: You are positioned to make a positive impact hundreds of years after you're gone.

so well, that even if you're gone for a few weeks, a few months, or even a year, it's just as profitable or more so than when you left. Between your family being empowered and working/planning well with your business team, you are positioned to be making a positive impact on others 2-3 generations, or even hundreds of years after you're gone.

This vision CAN BE your family's reality when you create and implement a great legacy plan.

LEGACY SCENARIO #2: THE ONE YOU'RE LIKELY HEADED FOR NOW:

Sadly, if you do what 90% of your successful peers do following traditional advice, here are the results you'll likely experience: your family experiences lots of strife due to time imbalance and lingering hurt feelings, and your children strug-

Where you're likely headed: family strife, anger, bitterness, your wealth squandered.

gle with bitterness and anger measuring their worth against your achievements. Your family falls apart after you're gone, fighting over the inheritance you leave them and prioritizing getting their "fair share" over maintaining good relationships with each other. Within one generation, two tops, all the wealth you built up is squandered and gone.

The charities you support waste **lots** of the money you give them, producing a very low social ROI and little impact to show for your contributions to them. In essence, your charity investments are **very** mismanaged, to the point that if the charities you work with were public companies, they'd be publicly shamed in the media for gross negligence of your funds.

Your business does not run well after you can no longer run it, to the point that it doesn't exist any more in the next 30-40 years due to mismanagement.

Your dreams of your business providing a better life for your family and your clients for multiple generations is not fulfilled.

In summary, in this scenario you'll have very little to show for all the hard work you put in to build your success, and you'll be forgotten by your family and others in only 2-3 generations.

Earlier I mentioned that it's essential you have accurate thinking about challenges you face. The sad fact of the matter is that there's a 90% chance you **will** experience scenario #2

> **Following traditional advice, you'll have very little to show for all the hard work you put in to building your success, and you'll be forgotten by your family & others in only 2-3 generations.**

above if you don't take action now to change your fate. Those are the cold, hard facts, and they must be addressed.

Lest you think this is all "the sky is falling" thinking or you're having a hard time believing this may be your family's fate should you stay on your current course, don't deceive yourself. These are the facts, and the sooner you accept your likely fate if you do what you've always done, the sooner you can choose a new fate for yourself, your business, and your family.

To drive this point home, let me tell you my OWN story and how the lack of intentional legacy planning affected me and my family...

> **Don't deceive yourself. The sooner you accept your likely fate if you do what you've always done, the sooner you can choose a new fate for yourself, your business, and your family.**

My mom and dad had sex once at the end of high school, were never married, and my dad isn't listed on my birth certificate. My mom married my stepdad when I was 5 days old, and I loved him dearly as a boy. After a difficult 5 year legal battle, he was approved to adopt me when I was 6, and shortly after that he told me he wasn't going to adopt me.

This rejection was so devastating to me that I blacked out all memories of my life up until that point, and even today I can only remember a few incidents that happened before age 7. I was very bitter towards my stepdad after he and my mom divorced when I was 7 because of the things I suffered: personal abandonment, emotional trauma, rejection, and the destruction of our home through his unfaithfulness to us all. At age 13 I forgave him and felt a massive weight lift off my shoulders. At that point, I thought I had moved past the hurt of rejection from my step-dad, but later I would find out that wasn't the case.

I met my birth father when I was 8, and he told me when I was 12 that, if I wanted to, we could get the paternity blood test to prove he was my father. Part of me wanted to get the test, but a bigger part of me thought, "What if he isn't my real dad?" As I thought of that potential letdown, my heart couldn't bear the thought of finding out I wasn't his, so I said no.

My identity of being rejected manifested in anger and rebellion in several ways, and by age 16 I had been arrested multiple times for stealing my mom's cars. I was quite suicidal at the time because I hadn't been able to stop stealing despite 2 years of effort to stop, and I was tired of trying to be a "good" child.

I became a Christian to see if it would help me stop stealing. Despite my pessimism that it would help me, I never had the urge to steal again after the day I became a Christian. The other huge benefit I got was that for the first time I felt like I belonged to a loving father figure. This may seem trivial to you, but to me it was a BIG deal. What does this part of my story have to do with you and YOUR legacy? A lot, actually. Please allow me to explain.

*Rejection is something that most children of successful people like you deal with. It has **lots** of negative consequences,* which may lead to alcohol and drug abuse or other addictions and destructive behavior. The good news is that in the next few pages I'm going to show you how to address this powerfully to help your children feel accepted and valued.

> # Rejection is something that most children of successful people like you deal with.

In my own experience, simply having someone to tell myself "that's my dad" helped me tremendously, as God is referred to as a Heavenly Father and Abba ("Daddy") in the Bible. Yet I still had other 'dad issues' to work through.

As an adult, I got laid off from my first full-time job at age 22 as a newlywed, and I went into business soon afterwards, realizing that job security only exists in your mind. By age 32, I was semi-retired with 8 different income streams, I published my first book, and I bought my 6 yr. old son his dream car, a red 1994 Lamborghini Diablo.

Within 2 years of 'arriving' I lost $500,000 on several bad investments, and afterwards I asked myself, "Why did I take such big risks?"

Within 2 years of 'arriving' I lost $500K on several bad investments, and afterwards I asked myself, "Why did I take such big risks with these investments?" After several years of self-study, coaching, and reflection, I figured out that I was driven to succeed in business so I could prove my worth to my two dads. At the age of 38, I realized I still wanted to be validated by them! Crazy, right?

In my studying about what drove me to succeed and what drives other successful people, I found out that often the root is a desire for validation. For many people, this comes from a childhood wound of rejection. This source of being driven, if not addressed strategically, often leads to a driven parent investing a lot of time in their business, and not investing enough time with their family, thus passing on the legacy of rejection to their *own* children.

A childhood wound of rejection often leads to a driven parent not investing enough time with their own children.

That was my experience. In looking at how I operated in business for 17 years, I was modeling my stepdad's workaholic patterns, spending very little time with my two sons and my wife. Once I started addressing these heart issues that drove me, I was able to operate from a place of being loved, accepted, and approved, and I started investing a lot more time with my wife and children. The change in my relationship with my children has been remarkable, and after reading this book, you'll know **exactly** how to model these new powerful results with your family as well. :)

There's two things I want you to take away from my story and this introduction:

1. To change your family legacy, it's key to openly admit what you're dealing with. Most men are taught that it's not 'manly' to share feelings of sadness or fear, and it's my belief that denying our feelings of hurt, sadness, and disappointment imprisons us.

> # You've made too many sacrifices to attain your success, only to throw it all away due to poor communication.

Most successful men have stuffed negative feelings deep down inside, and statistics show that 90% of their families fail long-term mainly due to poor/incomplete communication about personal issues. Following the Walt Disney rule to see what 90% of 'normal' people do and then doing the opposite, I say "forget that!" to the 90% family failure rate. That's not going to be the legacy I pass on to my family, and it's not how I want to be remembered. *My boys and my wife deserve better, and so do you, your family, and your team. You've made too many sacrifices to attain your success, only to just throw it all away due to poor communication, planning, and execution.*

2. You're not the only one dealing with the challenges you face. The more you're willing to deal with these deeper root issues, the bigger breakthroughs you, your family, and your whole team will experience. There are people you can open up with about the deeper issues of your life without fear of being judged (like me and my team), so you have all the tools and support you need to transform your family's legacy in your hands right now.

> **You're not the only one dealing with these challenges. There are people you can open up with... to transform your family's legacy.**

My desire is that you will read this book and find empowerment to avoid Scenario

#2 above. I will work alongside of you to help you achieve a legacy that makes life better for you, where all of your hard work building your business is continued in the next few generations.

There's no time to waste; keep reading to begin creating your new, lasting legacy now!

CHAPTER 1

Avoid Financial Success Failure. Say What?!?

In the introduction, I had you visualize 2 different futures for your family. You're successful, so I'll get right to the point and give your time the respect it deserves.

To begin with, I want to share a shocking yet very real risk you face, and how to address it: your success will most likely cause you and your family to fail.

I *know* it sounds crazy, but it's the truth. In fact, *the more successful you are, the **more** likely it is that your success will lead to failure for you and your family.* **I call this Financial Success Failure.**

The **good news** is this can be fixed, and in a moment I'll show you how to avoid this fate. :-)

Here are the 2 things you must now address to avoid Financial Success Failure:

1. **LACK OF KNOWLEDGE (heart issues)**

It's not your fault that your success has been contributing to or causing failure in your family thus far; no one has bothered to educate you about it!

Let's fix this now.

To start with, the reason you build your wealth and your business is to make a better life for your family and yourself, right?

Success will most likely cause you and your family to fail.

Growing up in poverty as I did or without nice things can be a powerful motivation to give your children a better life, and if you're not intentional about how you balance your business commitments and family time, it'll end bad for you just about every time. **Generally, the *more* successful you are, the more you work and the *easier* and *more likely* it is for**

distance to grow between you and those you love & care for.

The result of this is often heirs feel neglected and not important, and successful parents feel guilty and attempt to make up for missed time with their family by giving them gifts and privileges.

Despite the gift giving, usually your children will develop more anger, bitterness, and an orphan spirit the more you work and the more successful you become. (An 'orphan spirit' means feeling rejected, abandoned, and unloved like orphans feel.) *This is not what you want!*

The more successful you are, often your children will be angry & bitter.

In my own life, I experienced this phenomenon with my step dad. He worked very long hours and bought me lots of toys to make up for not being around to spend time with me very much. I came to believe work and material things were more important to him than I was, and I grew very angry and rebellious as a result. By the time I was 16, I was stealing cars to get my dad's attention so he'd spend some time with me... even if it was going to court with me.

If you **don't** address this Success Failure issue in your own family, your family will continue to be harmed by your wealth, and no matter **how** much money you leave them as an inheritance, it won't make up for their hurt **nor** will it empower your family long-term.

> # If you don't address 'Success Failure,' your family will be harmed by your wealth

2. LACK OF PROPER PREPARATION (wrong asset focus)

The second factor that leads to Financial Success Failure is lack of training and preparation for your family to manage what you leave them.

Again, most vendors drop the ball **big-time** when it comes to this. No matter how good your estate plan is and how advanced your tax-saving plan is to reduce your inheritance tax, your family will **still** have a 90% chance of failure financially after you're gone. Why is this?

The reason why is that 99% of the estate planners and asset protection attorneys that you turn to are focused on the **wrong** thing when it comes to helping you... leading to a 90% failure rate.

Now that you're aware of how an orphan spirit and lack of proper preparation will lead you and your family to Financial Success Failure unless you **proactively** do something different, I have great news for you: you can begin to fix these issues **fast!**

Follow these steps to avoid Financial Success Failure:

1. **Shift your focus to now, not when you die.** Traditional estate plans focus on keeping taxes to your estate low, yet they don't deal with the heart issues mentioned above.

Since I'm not an estate planner, I can address heart issues many other advisors may be hesitant to bring up to you for fear that you might be offended and won't do your estate plan with them. I

> **Since I'm not an estate planner, I can address heart issues many other advisors may be hesitant to bring up for fear that you may be offended.**

have no licensure restrictions and I operate by King Solomon's philosophy that "wounds from a friend can be trusted.[1]" As I consider you a friend (although perhaps a very new one), I care for you enough to tell you truths that may offend you or be very hard to hear.

Please trust me enough to share some very hard truths with you that you need to hear, and know when you let yourself be challenged, that's where breakthroughs occur in your life.

With that understanding in place, here's the truth:

If you follow the traditional route, distance will remain in your family, and your heirs will likely wait for you to die to get their inheritance.

When these heart issues aren't addressed, often your children will "act up" to get attention like I did at 16 stealing cars, or they will go wild like Paris Hilton and bring shame and stress to your family.

Traditional Estate planners will advise you to put provisions in trust

> **Please trust me enough to share some hard truths with you; when you let yourself be challenged, breakthroughs can occur.**

funds that your heirs only get their inheritance from you provided they act a certain way. There are two big weaknesses to this approach: 1. it uses money to control others, so it creates more distance in your family, and 2. it **also** doesn't prepare your heirs to wisely handle money or carry on your legacy at **all**. The first step to fix this is to **transform** your definition of what an inheritance is, and to pass it on to them **now**, not when you die.

Transform your definition of inheritance, and pass it on NOW, not when you die.

2. **Redefine inheritance** King Solomon, the richest man that ever lived, said "A good man leaves an inheritance to his children's children.²" Almost everyone thinks an inheritance is the money and assets you pass on to others. With this definition, then the most logical question becomes "How much should I pass on to my heirs to help them and not hurt them?" This is what many Giving Pledge members³ are discussing with each other; how much of an inheritance is too much? How do we avoid our children ending up like Paris Hilton,

or becoming lazy bums their whole life because they don't have to work?

These are important questions to ask, and they only address **part** of what an inheritance is. When you shift your definition of what an inheritance is, it leads you to ask **much** more empowering questions and allows you to pass on your inheritance right away.

Shift your whole approach from death planning to LIFE planning for your family.

Here's what a true, lasting inheritance is:

The values, skillsets, and life lessons passed on to your heirs, that the financial assets you leave them merely support them in living out. When you shift your focus to leaving your heirs a **lasting** inheritance, your whole approach shifts as well from 'death planning' to '**life** planning' for you and your whole family. Instead of asking "How much money should we leave to Billy and Sarah?" you can start asking "How do we most effectively pass on our values, skills, and life lessons to Billy and Sarah so they can NOW live life most abundantly?" This shift in focus is truly **life**-changing!

To maximize the positive effects of leaving a lasting inheritance to your family, you must do 2 things:

A) discuss/teach your values, skills, and life lessons with your family regularly, and...

B) live them out consistently.

To drive home the vitality of both components, I'll share a true-life story with you. King Solomon left his son a $1.5 Trillion fortune at his death. This is no exaggeration - Solomon owned several gold mines in addition to other business ventures, and *his gold holdings alone were worth $1.5 Trillion.*[4]

To put his wealth in perspective, he was worth the equivalent of the combined net worth of the Forbes 400 list members. It's truly a staggering financial inheritance, isn't it!

Because King Solomon's son did not apply wisdom to managing his business ventures well, he squandered much of his father's wealth and

King Solomon left his son a $1.5+ Trillion fortune - the equivalent of the Forbes 400 list's total wealth!

a couple generations later his family's gold business wasn't even in operation. In fact, the family had done such a poor job of passing on their skillsets that Solomon's great grandson couldn't even get the ships down to the port where their gold mines were located when he attempted to restart the family gold business!!

What went wrong? Solomon left his son **lots** of written instructions on how to be wise in business, which we still have today in the books of Proverbs and Ecclesiastes. So it wasn't for lack of instruction. *I believe the reason why Solomon's son squandered his wealth was he didn't see his father model diligence enough in his later years, and he modeled his dad's behavior.*

> ## Solomon built the largest palaces, had 800 wives, and had every vehicle and toy known to man- he experienced every known pleasure the world had to offer.

To use modern-day parlance, Solomon got fat and happy. He built the largest palaces in the world, had 700 wives and 300 live-in mistresses, and had every vehicle and toy known to man. With his level of wealth, he basically experienced every pleasure the world had to offer in his lifetime. Pleasure is great to enjoy, and pleasure for pleasure's sake isn't fulfilling long-term. After all the pleasures he experienced, Solomon said at the end of his life "all is vanity and chasing after wind[5]" meaning 'all the work I've done and all the pleasures I've experienced haven't fulfilled me long-term.' *For our heirs to carry on a powerful, positive legacy for us, it's vital that we both teach them **and** show them how diligently working hard and smart preserves the wealth we enjoy.*

3. **Pass on your inheritance NOW.** No, I'm not saying pass all your $ on to your children now, leaving yourself penniless and dependent on them to survive. So go ahead and breathe a sigh of relief. :) *What I'm referring to is developing and implementing a gameplan to pass on your values, skills, and lessons learned to your family beginning now so that they're empowered to carry out your vision for many centuries to come!*

Pass on your values, skills, & lessons now.

There are 4 main steps involved in doing this:

Step 1 - create a Family Mission Statement and Family Vision Statement.

Step 2 - host a Family Vault Meeting, passing on life lessons learned yearly.

Step 3 - set up a Family Vault Counsel that makes important family decisions together.

Step 4 - host ongoing Family Vault Meetings 1-2 times/year to enrich your family **long**-term.

With diligence and the right approach, you'll create a new, positive legacy of success.

Determine for yourself that your family will NOT fall victim to Financial Success Failure, and develop a gameplan to empower your family to carry out your vision for many centuries to come.

WARNING!

YOU ARE ABOUT TO READ A CHAPTER THAT
WILL LIKELY CHALLENGE YOUR BELIEFS
ABOUT WHAT'S POSSIBLE FOR YOU.

REMEMBER THAT TRADITIONAL THINKING
HAS BEEN INGRAINED IN YOUR MIND, AND
YOU MAY HAVE A KNEE-JERK REACTION
TO SOME OF THE STATEMENTS AHEAD.

I HAVE ONLY ONE REQUEST: WHEN YOU
READ SOMETHING AND YOUR
INITIAL REACTION IS
"That's Not Possible!"
SIMPLY ASK YOURSELF
"HOW can that be possible?"

AS YOU NOW READ THIS CHAPTER WITH
A MIND OPEN TO NEW POSSIBILITIES,
YOU WILL GET MAXIMUM BENEFIT
OUT OF YOUR READING.

LET'S GET TO IT!

CHAPTER 2

For "Manly Men" Only

To create a legacy of lasting success for your family, it's **vital** that you go to the level of leadership teaching and guiding your family; this requires new understandings and upgraded commitments.

If you do what most people around you do, you'll get the same results they do. A greater than 50% chance of getting divorced, a 76% chance your heirs will run your business into the ground within 25 years of you handing it over to them, and a 90% chance your grandkids will blow any wealth that's left that your heirs pass on to them.

Are you ready to step up your leadership to avoid this fate? Are you ready to be the man that takes your family and your business to lasting success? Great!

That's exactly what's required. But what does it mean to 'be the man' anyways?

"Be tough. Be strong. Don't be a wimp." These are all messages taught to men.

Men are taught from society what manliness is from a young age. Although each culture is different, in developed countries there are many commonalities about what is considered manly.

Here are some of the key things taught to most boys about how to be a man: "Be tough. Be strong. Defeat your opponent. Never show fear. Never show weakness. Big boys don't cry. Don't be a p*ssy. Don't be a wimp. Quit acting like a little b*tch. Man the f*ck up. Be a man." These are all messages taught to men, and I'm sure you've heard at least half of them from male role models in your life.

The only negative emotions most men feel comfortable showing to others are disappointment and anger.

Most men don't feel safe expressing sadness, worry, and fear, lest they be called a wimp or worse.

We're taught to keep these emotions to ourselves, which isolates us and makes us unable to communicate effectively with others.

How did we get to this place where men are so emotionally isolated and impotent? Garrett White, in "The Problem" chapter of his Warrior Book (www.WarriorBook.com), gives a great history lesson on what's happened to men in the last couple centuries since the Industrial Revolution began:

In the Agrarian age, both mom and dad spent time as a family unit teaching, guiding, and raising their children on their farm. It was common for children to work in the field with their dad, and there was a close relational bond as a result. When the Industrial Age came along, families moved to the city, and men left home, worked at the factory, and came home tired.

> **We're taught to keep these emotions to ourselves, which isolates us and makes us unable to communicate effectively with others.**

This had 2 effects on men: their creativity was stifled and punished, and since they worked long hours away from home, they functioned like an ATM for their family- providing great income for the family and little more.

The next thing that shifted the role of men in society was WWI, where men were taught that in order to follow orders and survive in battle, they had to suppress their feelings.

In WW I, men were taught that in order to survive in battle, they had to suppress their feelings.

While this survival mechanism worked great during wartime, after WWI men still lived with the mindset that 'sharing feelings isn't safe, so don't feel,' and after WWII women were used to working outside the home.

Lastly, feminism started out as women wanting equality with men, and with artificial insemination it morphed into a message of "we don't need you" being sent to men. This has led to confusion among boys and men about what it means to be a man, and what's expected of men today.

This confusion has led to the extended adolescence we see among men today, that are content to live at home with their parents well into their 20s, playing video games and delaying the age that they take full responsibility for their lives.[1]

Knowing these trends of the past 150 years or so has created massive confusion about what manhood is, I ask you the question: What does it mean to be a man? In your work, in your marriage, with your children, with others, with your contribution to the world? Have you defined it? Or have you let others define it for you? If you've let others define it for you, like most guys do, it's ok; that's the most logical thing to do when you're confused.

> **What does it mean to be a man? In your work, in your marriage, with your children, with others, with your contribution to the world?**

I encourage you to define what you want in life in every area, and be humble enough to admit where you are now, including in areas of your life where things are lacking.

The "Be, Do, Have" formula doesn't just apply to business; it applies to everything. In order to transform your results in the areas of your life that are less than ideal, you need to look at who you're being in those situations, and be willing to change.

This will require you to be honest about where you came from, and to be willing to upgrade your definition of manhood.

In the past couple of pages, we've covered how men have been conditioned by society to think and act certain ways, mainly that sharing feelings isn't safe. The other main factor that contributes to how you show up in life, in addition to societal conditioning, is modeling. You'll usually model the behavior of the men that were most influential in your life- those you spent the

> # The other main factor that contributes to how you show up in life, in addition to societal conditioning, is modeling.

most time with. In a moment, I'm going to show you how looking at where I came from and what behavior I was modeling helped me turn things around and first it's vital for you to know three main concepts King Solomon teaches that will help you transform your life as well.

> **If you don't listen to others and only do what you think is the right thing, you'll end up making deadly mistakes.**

1. "Pride comes before a fall, yet humility comes before honor.[2]" Be humble, admit where you are, and seek/listen to good counsel and advice.
2. "Wounds from a friend can be trusted.[3]" True friends will tell you the truth in love, even truths that wound you when you hear them because they're so painful.
3. "There is a way that seems right to a man, yet in the end it leads to death.[4]" If you don't listen to others and only do what you think is the right thing, you'll eventually end up making deadly mistakes.

Earlier I shared with you how my stepdad choosing not to adopt me caused me to block out most memories of my life before age 7, to adopt an orphan spirit of rejection, and to spend the next 30 years trying to prove my worth to him, including taking many risks in business that cost me over $500,000 in 2008.

Now, I'm going to share with you things from my past I have only told a handful of people, and that I have certainly never put in print. This is to show you the power of modeling, and to help you look at your life and your past with eyes wide open. It was only through looking at my life, humbly admitting what wasn't working,

The Legacy I was given: My grandparents committed adultery on each other, & my stepdad committed adultery on my mom- even bringing prostitutes home to sleep with when my mom was there.

and asking for input, that I discovered these things.

The Legacy I was Given and Modeled:

1. Adultery: There was lots of adultery in my family. My grandparents committed adultery on each other, leading to multiple divorces. My stepdad committed adultery on my mom- even bringing prostitutes home to sleep with when my mom was there- and gave my mom venereal diseases twice. He was married 8 more times after my mom, and repeated the pattern for many years.

I repeated his bad habits, getting hooked on pornography as a teenager, and continuing to indulge in it and flirting with other women for the first 15 years of my marriage. I told myself it was ok and I was being a good husband as long as I didn't physically sleep with other women, and that was a lie.

> **I repeated my stepdad's bad habits, getting hooked on pornography as a teenager, and flirting with other women for the first 15 years of my marriage.**

2. Verbal abuse and rejection: My grandparents told my mom and her siblings almost daily, "You're ugly," "I hate you," and "No one will ever love you." In addition to flirting with other women and sleeping around on her, my stepdad told my mom that if she ever told anyone about his partying with drugs and hookers, that he'd kill her. My mom modeled my grandmother and accused/character assassinated all 3 of her

> **My grandparents told my mom almost daily, "You're ugly," "I hate you," and "No one will ever love you."**

husbands when she got angry, and I ended up marrying a woman that went into accusation mode and made threats when she got angry. Up until 6 years ago, I would threaten divorce with my wife when we had big arguments as well.

3. Murder: My grandfather and grandmother fought daily, verbally, and often physically, and eventually my grandfather murdered my grandmother in front of my mom, choking her to death. Fortunately he knew CPR, and he revived her after a couple minutes of my mom looking at him. My first stepdad attempted to

murder both of his sons when my mom was pregnant with them; my 1st brother was born 3 months early and survived, and my second brother died in my mom's womb at 8 months old. During her C-section, my mother died 3 times on the operating table due to blood loss, and they were able to revive her.

I exhibited many of the signs of a serial killer when I was 4-6 years old, taunting other children and torturing animals; once I tried to drown a cat, which had to be rescued by a sewer worker. It is only by God's grace that my mom made me memorize Bible verses on how to deal with my anger productively, or else I'd likely be in prison for murder myself. The Bible verses worked so well, I've never even been in a fistfight, if you can believe that! Why do I tell you all this? First, it's powerful to understand your struggles. The first time I got a $20,000 check in business, my first impulse was to go to a strip joint and party with some strippers.

My first stepdad attempted to murder both of his sons when my mom was pregnant with them.

I remember beating myself up thinking, "Why do I want to party with strippers instead of celebrating this win with my family?" Once I understood my stepdad and grandpa's actions, it all made sense that I was tempted to model them, carrying on the family legacy of adultery.

Second, it's freeing to share your deepest, darkest secrets and remove the shame that comes with them. As long as you hide something, it can keep you in the dark, afraid others will find out about it. Bringing it out into the light exposes it and weakens its' power over you. *I want you to experience the same freedom I do* when I share my past with others, so you and others can all benefit.

Lastly, talking about your past hurts and struggles allows you to know you're not alone and to receive help from others. Many men are taught that asking for help means you're weak, and that goes against

I remember beating myself up thinking, "Why do I want to party with strippers instead of celebrating this win with my family?"

their belief, "Don't show weakness." As long as you share your challenges with mature men that want to help you improve your life, sharing them openly will help you overcome them fast.

Now that we've covered societal conditioning and modeling others' behavior, you know how you came to define manhood. Based on what I lived with, my definition of manhood before I decided to improve my life was:

"A man works hard and enjoys the fruits of his labor, and as long as he's paying the bills he can do what he wants. A man should play with his children, and wives should take care of the house. A man gets his woman to do what he wants by flirting with other women and threatening to leave her. A man figures out how to deal with problems, and only asks for help in extreme emergencies. A man reveals as little of his weaknesses as possible, so he isn't rejected."

Talking about your past hurts and struggles allows you to know you're not alone and to receive help from others.

I didn't **consciously** tell myself this, and it's the 'manhood' definition I lived by. It's ugly, I know. Living by this definition of manhood led me to keep my fears, sadness, and concerns inside, which isolated me. My isolation led to my porn addiction getting worse, and to me figuring out how to deal with business challenges on my own. This led to me losing $500,000 when the real estate market crashed in 2008, and to a loss of trust and intimacy with my wife.

> # The 'manhood' definition I unconsciously lived by led to me to losing $500,000 when the real estate market crashed in 2008, and to a loss of trust and intimacy with my wife.

How did I solve these dilemmas? I found some mature men that I could admit my challenges to, and asked them for help.

In 2010, I met a guy named Steve at a business meeting; I asked him what was new, and he told me that he was going to a men's accountability group to help him overcome addiction to pornography to strengthen his marriage. My reply? "I need to come to that!" I started going to local Celebrate Recovery (CelebrateRecovery.org) meetings, and for the next 9 months I had **complete** victory over porn; over 80% of men struggle with porn, and you **can** consistently have victory in this area of your life.[5]

Through this dramatic 180 degree turnaround in my life and sharing the journey with other powerful men, I discovered that *the opposite of addiction isn't sobriety; it's **connection***.

> # For 9 months after joining CR, I had COMPLETE victory over porn; the opposite of addiction isn't sobriety; it's CONNECTION.

I've asked you twice in this chapter: what is a man? By now, you know that we're not in the fields killing our fellow man for a living like during the world wars, so we don't need the emotional barriers any more. Also by now, you know that we're meant to be WAY more than just a paycheck for our families. *Knowing this, how do we overhaul our life so we can experience deep connection again? By first redefining what it means to be a manly man, and then by getting support.*

Since 'traditional manhood' leaves 90% of families falling apart and failing, let's simply turn everything on its head and do the opposite of what we've done so far, redefining what manhood is for us and our families. That leaves us with this definition of a manly man:

> **What is a man? We're meant to be WAY more than just a paycheck for our families.**

"A real man provides for and protects his family, and connects with them emotionally. He shares ALL his emotions in a productive way– including sadness, worry, and fear- in order to deal with life powerfully. A real man admits weaknesses with those that care about him so he can get help and support where and when he needs it."

Wow. We just redefined manhood...that's a BIG deal!

A real man provides for and protects his family, and connects with them emotionally. He shares ALL his emotions in a productive way in order to deal with life powerfully.

Feel free to add items to your personal definition that incorporate your personal and family's values as well.

Due to my upbringing, at age 18 I committed to giving my children the stability I never had- to staying married and to living in the same city, so they could have the same friends at school, at church, and in our neighborhood. A few years ago I realized I had kept those commitments, yet it's not good enough to do better than my stepdad's horrible example. I've moved the needle from abuse to neglect, and the next level I'm committed to is nurturing my wife and communicating openly with her and others.

To help you make your own powerful definition of manhood, I encourage you to do the following:

1. Write down who and what you're committed to being and achieving.

2. Write down areas you're weak in that you want to improve (even if you don't know how yet). If you don't know

At age 18, I committed to giving my children the stability I never had.

why you do certain things, that's ok. Maybe your parents aren't around to tell you where certain patterns came from; the key thing is to be brutally honest with yourself and write down what areas of your life aren't working as well as you want them to.

3. Write out what you're committed to that's the opposite of the items you wrote in #2, and state them in the present tense. (example: "I am a great provider, protector, and lover of my wife.")

One person I've been inspired by that I **highly** recommend you study and model is Peter Daniels. He was an illiterate 3rd generation welfare recipient and a bricklayer in his 20s, and after deciding to follow Jesus at a Billy Graham crusade in 1956, he taught himself to read and was mentored by a successful man for 6 years on Saturdays.

He asked God what he should do with his life, and the question came to him, "How much money can you give away in your lifetime?" This led to him going into business, and despite his first 4 ventures ending in bankruptcy, his 5th venture became a resounding success. Mr. Daniels and his family have given away multiple millions, and he has a vision to inspire other entrepreneurs to model

Mr. Daniels has a written plan for the next 5 generations of his family to carry out.

him so they can collectively give over $50 Billion to charities.

Further, Mr. Daniels has a written plan for the next 5 generations of his family to carry out. A vision of this scope **requires** that you get buy-in from your whole family and think long-term about your legacy, and I encourage you to expand your vision to think 5 generations ahead in your family's legacy plans like Mr. Daniels has! Discover more about him at www. PeterJDaniels.com.

Let's bring this chapter to a close with the following best practices to get support on your journey of living as a renewed, fulfilled, and powerful man:

A) **Recite your new definition of a manly man regularly,** until you know it by heart and believe it. Say it aloud with strong feeling for a month or two daily, pretending that you're auditioning for a movie role and want to convince others you believe it. Even though you likely won't believe it at first, repeating it to yourself regularly with feeling will cause you to start believing it over time.

> **Recite your new definition of what a manly man is regularly, until you know it by heart and believe it.**

B) **Practice vulnerability.** Sharing weaknesses shows you're not alone, and allows help to come so things can improve. This is rarely easy at first; it took me 3 months to write out my mistakes the first time I did it in Celebrate Recovery. Start by writing things you want to improve out on paper, then share them with mature, supportive friends and wise advisors. *Billionaire Elon Musk is very selective about who he spends time with, and one of his main criteria is whether a person will give him constructive criticism when he asks for input, even if they think he won't like what they have to say.[6] *Model Elon and only hang out with people who love you enough to speak hard truths to you and hold you accountable to keep stepping up your game.*

> # Model Elon Musk and only hang out with people who love you enough to speak hard truths to you.

C) **Find mature men to share life with that will help you grow.** Celebrate Recovery meetings can help you deal with addictions and co-dependency powerfully, and MasterMind meetings are great to hone your business and family legacy strategies.

As you likely know, it can take a **long** time to search in your local networks- work, church, friends, etc. – to find other men that are willing to open up and grow along with you.

How do I know this? Because I searched for men to mentor me in several areas of life, and it was a multi-year search that cost me hundreds of thousands of dollars, often filled with frustration that very few men were willing and able to help me.

To help **you** save lots of wasted time, money, and frustration finding other like-minded businessmen that are committed to living an abundant life in all areas, and to growing fast with raw honesty and vulnerability, I encourage you to use the following resources:

> # I searched for men to mentor me in several areas of life, and it was a multi-year search that cost me hundreds of thousands of dollars, often filled with frustration.

1. Apply to attend a LegacyBuilders retreat. These are held a few times/year with only 30-40 men. Full details at www.BeyondBillions.com/retreats

2. For stronger support, apply for LegacyBuilders group coaching where you'll optimize your life and family legacy monthly with 4-6 other successful men in a powerful, supporting environment. Full details: www.BeyondBillions.com/GroupCoaching

3. For personal guidance that gives the fastest growth, apply for our LegacyBuilders 1-on-1 coaching. This is limited to only a few selected clients, and if you're ready to make a serious investment in transforming your and your family's legacy FAST, and you're 100% committed to creating these new results for your family, then apply at www.BeyondBillions.com/1-on-1Coaching

For personal guidance that gives you the fastest growth, apply for our Legacy-Builders coaching.

CHAPTER 3

"You're my BOY, Blue!!"

In the movie 'Old School,' several middle aged men look to prove to themselves and others that they're still cool by starting a fraternity for adult men on their local college campus.

One of the characters in the movie, Blue, is a Navy veteran in his 70s that pledges for the fraternity. The movie is full of hilarious hijinks, **and** it highlights a desire of every man: to prove that they're cool and desirable i.e. they're 'the man.'

What does this movie have to do with your family legacy? A lot, actually. In the last chapter, we intentionally defined how you want to live as a man, yet how do you know *when* you're a man? When others say you're doing a good job? When you feel you're doing OK? Without clarity on this point, you and your heirs will waste lots of energy and effort trying to PROVE that you're a man (just like good 'ole Blue did in 'Old School'), when there's a better way of knowing that you're a real man.

So, what is this better way? **Being affirmed.**

This affirmation can come in many forms. Looking throughout history, most cultures have had some sort of rite of passage or ceremony to accept young men and young women as adults in their community. For millennia, young men have had to hunt specific animals in many countries to become a man; the Greeks (as depicted in the movie '300'), the Ma'asi African tribe, and many American Indian tribes had/ have this as part of the passage into manhood.

In Jewish culture, when young men and young women reach the age of 13, they have a Bar (or Bat) Mitzvah ceremony where they recite a section of the Torah they have memorized, and they are then recognized and celebrated as young adults.

The fact that these ceremonies take on so many different forms, with different elements and requirements, shows that there is no one right way to hold a rite of passage/affirmation ceremony. What they all have in common is that a young man or woman is acknowledged and recognized as an adult.

In the last chapter, I talked about confusion many have when it comes to defining manhood. Further confusion exists around knowing when a young man is finally an adult. Ask 100 men age 25+ when they became a man, and you'll get **lots** of different answers. Some think it's when they got a car, when they got their first job, the first time they had sex, when they moved out of their parents' house, or many other life events. The point is that there's little agreement about when someone becomes a man.

I think we should model the ancient wisdom of most societies throughout history, and affirm our heirs to eliminate their confusion about whether they're a real man or woman with a ceremony. This will have the benefits of settling once for all that **they're adults**, will free them up from needing to prove themselves to others, and will greatly **strengthen your family**.

Whether your children are under age 13, or they're in their 50s and you're in your 80s, you and your family can benefit from applying this affirmation ceremony strategy. Let's go deeper into the benefits of holding these ceremonies, and then cover best practices for your ceremony and discuss different ways you can arrange it for each heir.

Ceremony Benefit # 1: Having a ceremony helps your heirs **know** that they're adults. This benefits your heirs greatly, because instead of wondering if they're an adult or not, they'll know they became an adult on a certain date. Not only is the date important; it's also important for them to know that you respect them as an adult, **and** that you value them and are proud of them just because they're yours... not because of their performance being "good," they agree to take over your family business, or some other action you desire for them to take.

Affirmation Benefit # 2: Affirming your heirs frees them from trying to prove themselves to you, which is a **big** deal when you're a multimillionaire or a billionaire and they feel pressure to "measure up" to you- both from you and from others. It's natural as a parent to want your children to do better than you, and to have a better life than you did. That's a healthy desire for progress.

At the same time, if you're not careful, this good desire can have bad consequences if your child isn't as talented as you in the area of business. If they feel they can't be as good as you, they may simply not want to even try to succeed at all. Instead of trying to compete with you, help your heirs run their **own** race where their only objective is to be the best they can be with their talents and abilities.

Because others will still compare your children to you, it's vital that you affirm them on an ongoing basis for doing their best while encouraging them to keep improving. This will remind them that they don't have to overwork themselves to please you, and will **greatly** improve your family relationships.

Ceremony Benefit # 3: When your heirs know they're adults and they know you are proud of them, your family communication and relationships will improve drastically. As mentioned in chapter 1, most successful families suffer from Financial Success Failure where the family's financial success lead to a breakdown of the family unit. A side effect of that phenomenon is that often heirs become jealous or resentful of their parent's business because it takes up so much of their time.

I personally know 2 business owners worth over $50 Million each whose adult children

> **I personally know 2 business owners worth over $50 Million each whose adult children won't speak to them.**

won't speak to them because they didn't affirm their heirs when they were children. They are living the "Cat's in the Cradle" song out in real life.

To avoid this fate of estranged heirs if your children still live with you, I recommend you follow Jim Sheils' recommendation in his book "The Family Board Meeting" to have quarterly meetings with each of your children one on one where they choose a fun activity for you to do for 4 hours, then you have a time to talk 1 on 1 and encourage them.[1] If any of your heirs are already estranged, affirming them is the #1 way to start healing your relationship with them.

Ed Mercer, serial entrepreneur billionaire, shows that it's possible to build better relationships with your heirs when they're well into adulthood. After growing up with a father that sexually abused him and his siblings regularly, and living in a house with no running water or electricity as a teenager after his dad died, Ed decided to be a success and buy the house he grew up in.

Ed Mercer, billionaire, shows that it's possible to build better relationships with your heirs when they're adults.

This decision led him to pour into personal development and by age 19 he bought the house he grew up in. From there, he became a real estate millionaire in his 20s and a billionaire in his late 30s.

Ed was married and had 2 children in his 20s, and one side effect of his modeling his dad's workaholic habits was that he didn't invest much time in his family while he was building his first business empire.

Like me, Ed wasn't content to merely move his family legacy from abuse to neglect, so he recently moved from Costa Rica back to Canada to live next door to his daughter and grandchildren. If Ed, a billionaire, can give up living in a tropical paradise to move back to the frigid North in his 70s to empower his children, you too can rebuild a better relationship with your heirs, no matter how old you are.

Now that we've covered the benefits of holding a ceremony to affirm your heirs and affirming them on an ongoing basis, let's cover best practices for doing your affirmation ceremony, whether your heirs are children or already adults.

> **If Ed can give up living in a tropical paradise to move back to the frigid North to empower his heirs in his 70s, you can do it too.**

*Here are the main steps involved in **now** affirming your heirs with a ceremony:*

Step 1- Choose the type of affirmation ceremony you want to have

There are 3 types of ceremonies you can have: men only for sons, women only for daughters, or coed with both parents participating. The benefits of a men/women only ceremony are that you can speak more freely about male and female-specific challenges (like hygiene, intimacy, etc). The benefits of a co-ed ceremony are that your whole family can attend, which allows for a more festive ceremony and for both parents to bless your child.

I recommend speaking with your heir and your spouse to determine the best type of ceremony to have; as its main purpose is to affirm your heir, do the type of

> **As its main purpose is to affirm your heir, do the type of ceremony they desire even if it's different than your or your spouse's preference.**

ceremony they desire even if it's different than your or your spouse's preference. If you're divorced and your ex doesn't want to participate or your spouse is deceased, it's good to know you can do your heir's affirmation ceremony many different ways.

Step 2- Choose the theme and location/date for your heir's affirmation ceremony

For most people that have an affirmation ceremony, they say it's one of the most important events in their life. As such, take the arranging of the ceremony seriously.

You don't need to spend thousands or 100s of thousands of dollars on the ceremony. However, treat it as an event that your heir will remember throughout their life as important, and make a serious investment in it within your budget. Whether you make the ceremony solemn and serious or fun and fes-

> **For most people that have an affirmation ceremony, they say it's one of the most important events in their life.**

tive is up to you, and again as this ceremony is for your heir, let them have the main say in the theme of the event, your budget permitting.

Step 3- Invite an Advisory Board to write out advice and guests to attend the event

Your heir's advisory board is a group of mature men or women that will serve a few key purposes: to share some words of wisdom with your heir at their ceremony, to give them a gift if they desire to, and to be available to give advice to your heir on an ongoing basis. The younger your heir, the more likely they'll need your help picking 2-4 people to approach and invite to be advisors to them.

After inviting and putting together their advisory board, the next step is to ask each advisor to write them some words of advice about being a successful man or woman. Feel free to invite friends of yours

> **Ask advisors and friends to write your heir words of advice about being successful, and read some of their letters at their ceremony.**

that aren't on their advisory board to write them some words of advice, and even if they can't attend the ceremony, you can choose to read some of their letters to your heir at their ceremony.

As most successful entrepreneurs have full schedules, schedule your heir's ceremony at least 60 days away so most people may attend.

Step 4- Pick a gift to give your heir

This gift is symbolic of adulthood and should be something special. It doesn't need to be ultra-expensive, yet it should have meaning. It can be a family momento you pass down, a nice watch, or something else that will be treasured by your heir.

I remember getting a paisley tie as a graduation gift from my pastor, and his letter that came with it saying every man should have a paisley tie in his wardrobe made me feel like a

Give your heir an affirmation gift that signifies maturity and adulthood, and explain the meaning of the gift so they'll appreciate it.

man. Get your heir something that signifies maturity and adulthood, and explain the meaning of the gift to them so they'll appreciate it.

Step 5- Hold the Affirmation Ceremony

There are a few key components I recommend you include in your heir's affirmation ceremony:

a) Open with a welcome and state the purpose of the event to recognize your heir as an adult. (As desired, add a prayer, any special music your heir wants sung, or special performance.)

b) As the parent, speak blessings over your heir and state your commitments to them. Bless them to be successful with their work, family, health, and overall life. If you ever cursed your child in the past (like "You'll never amount to anything," "You're always a screw-up," etc.), this is a perfect time to ask your heir's forgiveness for speaking unwisely and commit to blessing them going forward. Bless them to make great decisions as a responsible man or woman, and commit to give them advice and support when they ask for it as adults. Solomon says, "A word well spoken is like apples of gold in pictures of silver." (Prov 25:11) Choose these words wisely!

c) Your heir shares their commitments- to seek wisdom, to be responsible, and to make a positive impact on the world with their talents and abilities.

d) Select advisors share their advice with your child. If they aren't able to attend yet sent a letter, read the letter to your heir for them.

e) You and their advisors speak final blessings over your heir (and pray for them as desired).

f) After the final blessings/prayer, present your heir to the attendees as a man or woman.

g) After the ceremony is done, celebrate!!! Do this with your own style- either simple or lavish. One thing I **really** like that Jewish fathers do is walk behind their child and shout, "This is my son/daughter, in whom I am well pleased!" What an awesome way to affirm your child!

As each family situation is different, add to the above elements as your family desires. If you host a men only or women only ceremony, record it so it may be shared with your spouse (after it's been edited if need be). Then the ceremony can bless you and your heir for years to come.

To get more detailed strategies for hosting your heirs' affirmation ceremonies, I highly recommend you read the books "The Power of a Parent's Blessing"

by Craig Hill, and for men only or women only ceremonies, read "Boy's Passage, Man's Journey" or
"Girl's Passage, Father's Duty" by Brian Molitor.

*Here are a few great ways to help you get the
most out of your Affirmation Ceremonies:*

1. Don't be afraid to invite estranged relatives to the
   ceremony. In both Craig Hill and Brian Molitor's
   books, there are stories of fathers and sons that
   started talking for the first time in years after
   attending one of these ceremonies. The part
   where a parent asks a child's forgiveness for curs-
   ing them in the past is especially healing and
   often restarts communication among previously
   estranged family members.

2. If you are estranged from an heir and want to
   have an Affirmation Ceremony for them, have a
   trusted 3rd party bring the idea up to them. This
   can be one of their friends, a trusted relative, or a
   family friend from church, the neighborhood, or
   other social circle, or an advisor. Having a trusted
   3rd party bring up the idea of an Affirmation
   Ceremony to them is a great way to maximize
   your odds that they'll at least hear the idea out
   and consider it.

3. As well as for your heirs, consider having an
   Affirmation Ceremony for yourself. This can

help you go to the next level of success and contentment... even if you're already a billionaire. It's powerful to hear blessings and affirmations spoken over you audibly. If your parent(s) have already died, you can have a surrogate stand in for your father in your ceremony. They don't have to be older than you in order to bless you; to be a surrogate for your ceremony, the man needs to be mature and confident enough to speak a powerful ceremonial blessing over you. Those are the only 2 requirements!

In closing this chapter, I want to share 3 quick stories that show how vital diligence is when it comes to blessing your family no matter what challenges may arise. The first 2 stories concern conducting my oldest son's Affirmation Ceremony last summer.

First, once I decided to hold his ceremony, I needed to find a host and location. My pastor of 20 years didn't understand and wasn't willing to conduct the ceremony, and the Jewish rabbi I knew wasn't able to conduct it due to illness. My friend Pastor Tim agreed to conduct the ceremony, which was great because he had conducted several Affirmation Ceremonies before. The new church I was attending would only let me have the ceremony there if I used one of their in-house pastors to conduct it, so I ended

up renting a restaurant room to have Pastor Tim conduct the ceremony. Bottom line: it was a frustrating
process at times, **and** I got the ceremony scheduled
due to flexibility about with whom and where we held
it.

Second, my wife and I were going through a challenging time in our relationship at the time of my son's
scheduled ceremony, and she told me she wouldn't
participate in it. Although hurt, I accepted that's where
she was at emotionally, and I chose to be at peace with
it. I had planned a Craig Hill-style father and mother
blessing of our son, and at the last minute I had to
adjust the ceremony format to a father and advisors
blessing of my son using Brian Molitor's format.

Bottom line: my son's ceremony could have been
thrown off track easily had I focused on these letdowns
by people close to me. By focusing on the event's benefit to my son and staying 100% committed to affirming his manhood, we had an amazing ceremony that
was very powerful. *I encourage you to have the same
tenacity in affirming your heirs, no matter what
challenges may arise.*

The third story is regarding my **own** affirmation
ceremony. A few years ago, I met a wise elderly man
from Asia that told me he had done several "Father's
Blessing" ceremonies for men in place of their fathers
who were unable or unwilling to affirm and bless

them. After getting to know him, he offered to do such a ceremony for me over Skype, and I accepted his offer. Although I followed up 4 times over a 2 month period to schedule the ceremony, he never confirmed a date/time to conduct the ceremony, nor responded about the topic at all. Although disappointed, I found a wise peer of mine who was willing to do my affirmation ceremony... once I let go of the notion that it had to be someone older than me. Learn from my experience, and be flexible enough to allow your affirmation to come from someone the same age or younger than you, as long as they're wise and capable.

Now you know the power of affirming your heirs as adults, and how to arrange and conduct an Affirmation Ceremony for them. Your affirmation will help them stop trying to prove they're a worthy man or woman, and will help them channel their energies to being the most successful, fulfilled adult possible.

Schedule a few hours to plan out your oldest living heir's Affirmation Ceremony with them and your spouse now, and get it done in the next 2-6 months. If you have multiple adult children, have their ceremonies at least 6 months apart so that they each get to have their own special day. (The only exception to this rule is if you're terminally ill; in that case, bless them all at once in one grand ceremony as soon as possible).

With the solid foundation of living out and passing on a powerful definition of manhood to your heirs, and affirming them, you are ready to add the next piece that keeps your whole family on the same page so the new legacy you're intentionally building will last for multiple generations. Keep building!

AFFIRMATION BONUS STRATEGY:

In this chapter, we spent a **lot** of time on how to do your heir's Affirmation Ceremony, yet little time on how to affirm them on an ongoing basis. Here's the **best** way I've discovered to do this: Embrace your inner Jewish parent! :)

While Jewish people make up only 2% of America's population, they represent 16 of the 40 richest Americans and 25% of Nobel prize winners as well. Why are they so successful? I think I've found the reason why: they bless their children regularly.[2]

During Erev Shabbat, a meal to thank God for his provision and begin their weekly day of rest, the parents (usually the father) bless their children. **The parents bless their children to be wise and successful, which dramatically boosts their**

children's confidence, and leads to high levels of success as the Forbes 400 list reflects.

I recommend you begin modeling this strategy with your family right away! You can do it weekly, twice/month, or monthly; the important thing is to get into the habit of doing it regularly. I personally do it once/month with my two sons, and I schedule my blessing of them on the first Saturday of the month.

*For best results, schedule your blessing of your heirs, speak your blessings in the present tense ("I bless you to prosper in your work, your relationships, and your health"), and be as specific as possible. Shalom!

CHAPTER 4

Is Your Family's Success Built to Last?

E arlier in chapter one, I shared that if you follow traditional advice when it comes to your legacy and estate planning, you're 90% likely to experience Financial Success Failure, meaning your financial success will actually lead to failure for your family unless you empower your family with the right mindset and skills.

The solution to this is three-fold: choosing to be a most powerful leader and affirming your heirs (as we covered in the last 2 chapters), and redefining what inheritance is to you. A **lasting** inheritance is passing on your skills, values, and life lessons on to your family and your business team. Once you realize the money you leave behind only **supports** your family in enjoying the inheritance you leave them, the next step is to begin passing on your inheritance to others **now**.

*There are 4 main steps involved in passing on your inheritance, and it's **vital** you carry out these 4 steps ASAP the right way so your family's success you're working so hard to achieve will last.*

> **A LASTING inheritance is passing on your life skills to your family and your business team- begin passing on your inheritance to others NOW.**

Here are the 4 main steps involved in NOW creating a Lasting Legacy for your family:

Step 1 - create a Family Mission Statement (a.k.a. your "Family Vision Statement")

One of King Solomon's most famous sayings is "Where there is no vision, the people perish.[1]" This is true for whole nations, for individuals, and for families as well. To pass on your values to your family, the first step is to clearly define what you're about and your vision for your family's future. That way even if your children don't want to be involved in your business in the future, they'll understand your values and what you want your business to accomplish in the world. They'll also understand the impact you want to make in the world with your business and charity work.

> **To pass on your values, the first step is to clearly define what you're about and your vision for your family's future.**

I recommend you make an overall Family Vision Statement, and make ones for your business and your charity work as well. This way your family will know your wishes for using your wealth to positively impact the world long after you're gone.

I encourage you and your spouse to set aside at **least** *2 hours to discuss your values with each other, write them down, and craft your Family Vision Statement together.* If you're able, I recommend you have a 3rd party help you with this process, as often things about your childhood or your past that have shaped your view of the world come up in these discussions, and it helps to have a person outside your family ask you certain questions to really get to the heart of what matters. I'll give you a personal example to drive home how having a 3rd party help you create your Family Vision Statement is helpful. I am a **very** curious person and ask lots of questions (like most billionaires). Fortunately, my mom encouraged me to ask questions and patiently answered them, which has helped me a lot in business.

> # I recommend you make an overall Family Vision Statement, and make ones for your business and your charity work as well.

With my wife, however, often when I ask her questions she thinks I'm challenging her, and will get defensive. When other people she's not so close with ask her questions, she's more open to share her feelings without being defensive. The same dynamic works out in most close relationships (either spouses, siblings, or parent/child), so I recommend you have a 3rd party help you create your Family Vision Statement.

When I and my team help our clients with this, it often takes 2-4 hours to go through the process of creating their Family Vision Statement, and it's

Have a 3rd party help you to really get to the heart of what matters when creating your amily Vision Statement.

worth **every second**! The reason why is this is a statement you'll be sharing with your family regularly for **many** years to come!

It's like laying a foundation to build a beautiful mansion on- you want that foundation to be strong and solid so the structure doesn't crumble in future years. *Your family's legacy is **way** more valuable than any mansion you can build, so don't skimp on this step; lay a **solid** foundation for your family's future with a clearly defined and honed Family Vision Statement.*

It often takes 2-4 hours to go through the process of creating your Family Vision Statement, and it's worth EVERY SECOND!

Step 2 - host Family Vault Meetings, passing on life lessons learned regularly

A Family Vault Meeting is a meeting you have with your family regularly to 'deposit' your family's wealth into so your whole family can benefit from it most powerfully. As we discussed earlier, the most valuable assets you're depositing into your Family Vault are your values, skills, and lessons learned, **not** money.

However, just like a physical vault protects valuables from damage and theft, your Family Vault will protect your family from unnecessary mistakes and help them deal with challenges throughout life. Your wealth when managed well will empower your family, and your Family Vault will empower you in amazing ways!

So now that you know what a Family Vault is and its benefits, here are some best practices for your Family Vault Meetings **("FVM" hereafter):**

> **A Family Vault Meeting is a meeting you have with your family regularly to deposit your family's relationship wealth into.**

A) Get your whole family together as much as possible- even your grown children and their children. The more people that come to your FVMs, the more the whole family is enriched.

B) Your FVM should last a full day. As the meeting involves talking as a family, I recommend you break up the talk times into 1-3 hour chunks so everyone can take a break and stay focused. This is **very** helpful for your children especially. When I and my team facilitate Family Vault Meetings for clients, we break up the meetings into 2 days, mixing in fun activities for the family to do each day. This way the children stay engaged the whole time!

C) You should host your initial FVM as soon as possible. Even if your family is spread out, you should be able to host your first meeting within 6 months of writing out your Family Vision Statement; schedule it ASAP, and either summer or end of year holiday times can be perfect as often families get together at those times anyways. After your initial FVM, host them once/year on an ongoing basis so your family stays enriched.

> **The more people that come to your FVMs, the more the whole family is enriched.**

D) FVM Location- I **strongly** recommend you host your FVMs somewhere outside your normal routine. Don't host them at your house as there are too many distractions there, and if you host a FVM at one of your vacation houses or at a place you visit regularly, don't settle into your normal routines there. The point is to **focus** during the meeting times and avoid "routine" distractions, so going to a new place **or** at a different time than normal will help you and your family get the most out of your FVMs.

> **Host your FVM somewhere outside your normal routine. Don't host them at your house as there are too many distractions there.**

E) As I said in item 2B above, break up your FVMs into 1-3 hour sections to keep everyone engaged, especially the children. If you have younger children, you may want to limit talk times to 60-90 minutes, then have 10 minute breaks in-between. The main components of a FVM are Legacy Story time, Vault Deposits and Withdrawals, and your Family Vault Counsel meeting.

i) During the Legacy Story time, someone in the family tells the rest of the family about their life; this helps the others in the family understand the family member better, and especially for grandkids hearing about their grandparents' struggles to become successful, it helps them appreciate what they have and the sacrifices made to provide it.

> **The main components of a FVM are Legacy Story time, Vault Deposits and Withdrawals, and your Family Vault Counsel meeting.**

ii) During your Vault Deposits and Withdrawals, each member of your family shares what victories they've had, what skills they've honed or developed, what values they've honed/developed, and what lessons they've learned in the last year or since your last FVM.

iii) During your Family Vault Counsel meeting, your family will discuss important things that affect your family and makes decisions as a family on how to best carry out your Family Vision Statement both individually and as a whole. Important decisions are voted on regarding strategy, finances, charity work, and other items.

> **During your Vault Deposits and Withdrawals, each member of your family shares what victories they've had since your last FVM.**

*As staying on track, respecting everyone's opinion and allowing them to speak, and documenting everything shared in your FVMs so the whole family can benefit from it for many years to come are **essential elements** to having successful FVMs, I highly recommend you have a 3rd party person facilitate your first 1-2 Family Vault Meetings.*

Make sure the person that hosts your FVMs meets the following qualifications:

> **During your Family Vault Counsel meeting, your family makes decisions regarding strategy, finances, charity work, and other key items.**

1. they're trustworthy i.e. they'll keep your family's secrets to themselves (they must be willing to sign an NDA and honor it), 2. they're respectful, 3. they have a positive view of wealth i.e. they won't judge you **or** be afraid

of speaking truthfully to you because of your wealth, and 4. they have great people skills.

Step 3- set up a Family Vault Counsel that makes important family decisions together

For your first FVM, you'll set up a Family Vault Counsel ("FVC" hereafter). These are members of the family that will volunteer to discuss and facilitate the family making important decisions together. This FVC's purpose is to help each family member (over age 18) be involved in important decisions that affect the family as a whole and then individually, and it promotes family unity.

> **With a 3rd party facilitating your FVM, make sure the host is trustworthy, respectful, and they have a positive view of wealth.**

At your discretion, your family can deposit actual money into a bank account the FVC controls and use the funds to assist family members during times of need during the Family Vault Deposits and Withdrawals portion of your FVMs. If someone takes a loan out from the FVC, it's best to be for important emergencies or for purposes that strengthen the family. For example, if Billy wants a $50,000 loan, it'd be much wiser to give him that loan to start a business than to buy an exotic motorcycle.

Thinking of inheritance creatively modeling King Solomon's teaching that "A good man leaves an inheritance for his children's children,[2]" I know one man that put funds into a FVC account and bought each of his children a house when they got married.

> **A Family Vault Counsel is made up of members of the family that will facilitate the family making important decisions together.**

That way they could pay the house off at 0% back to the family instead of paying compound interest to a bank. Think of creative ways to empower your family with your FVC as well!

Step 4- host ongoing Family Vault Meetings 1-2 times/ year to enrich your family LONG-term.

> # I know one man that bought each of his children a house when they got married.

Once you've held your initial FVM and set up your FVC, the last step to sustaining maximum wealth in your family long-term is to have ongoing FVMs at LEAST once/year. To keep your FVMs fresh and valuable so family members will be excited to attend them yearly, **I recommend the following:**

A) Host them at different locations every year. One great way to do this is during your FVC meeting, vote as family on where you want to host your next FVM the following year so you're all on the same page.

B) Have a different person share their story during the Legacy Story time each year. Start with the parents/grandparents, then go down to the children, then the grandkids. If you have a very large family, by all means have 2-3 people share their story during this part of your FVM. Also, leave time for family members to ask questions at the end of peoples' stories and make comments; this way your family will grow to understand and appreciate each other at a much deeper level.

> **To keep your FVMs fresh and valuable, host them at different locations, and have a different person share their story each year.**

In closing for this message, I want to leave you with a few key elements to ensure your FVMs are successful:

1. What is said during the FVMs stays in the room unless the person that shares says you can tell others. This is essential so each family member feels safe to truly share their heart and to foster 100% trust in your family.

2. Prioritize the harmony and well-being of your family, especially when you disagree with others on things. Humility comes before honor, and pride comes before a fall. Stay humble, and your family will stay in harmony.

3. Allow everyone in the family a chance to speak, and do not interrupt each other; only one person speaks at a time. It's normal to have questions when someone's talking, so encourage everyone in the family to write down their questions and ask them when the person's done speaking.

> **What is said during the FVMs stays in the room unless the person that shares says you can tell others.**

4. Respect other people's boundaries, and don't blame or attack other family members. When sharing, talk about what you think and how you feel using "me" or "I" statements; instead of saying "you make me feel..." say "I feel upset because..." to stay away from blaming.

5. If you have unresolved issues with another family member, attempt to make amends with them before your next FVM or speaking 1 on 1 with them at FVMs. It's always good to start by asking forgiveness for any way you've wronged them, and ask how you can be at peace with them going forward. Again, humility and love can heal any wound!

> **If you have an unresolved issue with another family member, attempt to make amends with them before your next FVM.**

That's all for the Family Vision Statement and Family Vault meeting basics, friend! *When you follow the above protocol regularly, you'll create a Lasting Legacy for your family that is powerful and positive, that can last for MANY generations to come!*

I don't know about you, but I get excited just thinking about this. :) Get excited, schedule a time to write your Family Vision Statement with your spouse in the next couple weeks and "get 'er done," and schedule your first Family Vault Meeting with your family members within the next 3-6 months.

If you need or would like support with

> **If you follow the above protocol regularly, you'll create a Lasting Legacy for your family that is powerful and positive, that can last for many generations to come!..**

any of the above steps creating your Family Mission Statement and arranging/hosting your initial Family Vault Meeting, I and my team may be able to help you with our Legacy Builders services. To apply for our Legacy Builders services, either email us at Support@BeyondBillions.com, go to www. BeyondBillions.com/FamilyVault, or call/text us at +1.248.325.8872 to now request your initial consultation, and someone from our team will get back to you within 2-3 business days.

CHAPTER 5

Will your dreams DIE with you or not?

Please forgive me if this question seems too direct: **Will your dreams die with you?**

If you're like 90% of successful business owners, sadly the answer is yes.

I'll explain why you're headed for business failure long-term in a moment, and then I'll give you a solution to help you avoid this fate.

Why are you building your business? As discussed earlier in Chapter 1, like most business owners, I bet you're putting in the hours, blood, sweat, and tears because you want to make a **better** life for your family, yourself, and your clients, right?

Well, the problem is you're likely building an unsustainable business, meaning there's a 90% chance your business will die with you and your dreams will die along with it once you can no longer run your company.

Lest you're telling yourself, *"David, I'm young and I won't die for a long time, so this isn't a problem for me,"* let me tell you 2 quick stories to show you why you need to address this challenge NOW.

> # There's a 90% chance your business will die with you, and your dreams will die along with it, once you can no longer run your company.

REAL-LIFE STORY 1

Corey Rudl was a popular internet marketer in the early 2000s, and by his early 30s his business was doing several million/year in sales. Like me, Corey was an avid fan of exotic cars and an adrenaline junkie. As such, he raced sometimes on a track near his house. One day Corey's friend was racing his

Porsche Carrera GT with him in the passenger seat, crashed, and they both died (JUST like Paul Walker). Corey went from "top of the world" to gone instantly at age 34, leaving a wife behind and his company struggling to survive.

REAL-LIFE STORY 2

Recently Forbes ran an article about the family that owns U-HAUL.[1] It's very fascinating, and very sad. The man that started the company with his wife had 6 children with 2 wives, and by the 1970s, only 2 of them were working in the family business.

The other sons got involved, took over the company and kicked their dad out of it (he was declining mentally and mismanaging the company), and for 40 years the family's relationships have been strained.

> **Corey went from "top of the world" to gone instantly at age 34, leaving a wife behind and his company struggling to survive.**

This **whole** sad saga could have been avoided with just **one key** strategic shift on the dad's part.

To read how these 2 stories turned out and discover how you can now avoid these sad fates for your family, continue reading!

The solution to the risk of your dreams dying suddenly and your business not being able to live on without you is *an effective, well carried out Succession Plan.*

A succession plan is basically a written plan that maps out who will do what running your company (or companies if you have many) in your absence.

The solution to the risk of your business not being able to live on without you is an effective, well carried out SUCCESSION PLAN.

Here are the steps to now take to put your own personal successful succession plan in place:

Successful Succession Plan Step 1:

Identify 1-2 key people that can run your business in your absence. Pick the best people to approach to run your business based on their values, skills, and teachability. Make a list of people that are strong in these 3 areas, and I encourage you to consider a honest, teachable employee/manager over a more experienced yet willing to cut corners person.

> **Honesty, trust-worthiness, and teachability are WAY more important than experience when it comes to running your business.**

Honesty, trust-worthiness, and teachability are **way** more important than experience when it comes to running your business.

Once you have your list of potential successors, get advisors' input on who is best to approach first about being a successor for your business(es). If you are inclined, next pray about it for confirmation that who you have in mind is a good fit, then approach the potential successor(s) to see if they're interested in running your business(es).

If you're like most successful business owners, your first choice will be for your heirs to run your business. It's **vital** for the morale of your existing business team members that you make your heirs earn their titles in your company by doing their duties with excellence. Your goal should be for your heirs to learn how each department of your company works, and for them to develop the habits of hard work, responsibility, and humility. In order to integrate them into your business team most effectively, find an existing team member to take them under their wings and show them the ropes.

It's VITAL for the morale of your business that you make your heirs earn their titles in your company.

Follow these best practices with your heirs work-ing in your business:

a) Do **not** play favorites with your heirs, which will hurt morale in your company; hold them account-able to do excellent, quality work, and empower your managers to hold your heirs accountable just like they would with any other employee.

b) Start your heirs out working in your company in depart-ments that best match/utilize their skills and interests. The DISC and Kolbe tests will help you determine this most effectively.[2] You'll want them to work in all your company's departments eventually so they understand the whole business, **and** you can get them most interested in your business by starting them off in a department that they are most likely to enjoy/do well in.

> **Do NOT play favorites with your heirs. Hold them accountable to do excellent, quality work.**

Successful Succession Plan Step 2:

The next step is to train your successors in the work they will do in your absence. Any tasks that only you do in your company, show them how to do it, have them do the tasks with you reviewing them/being there to help if needed, then document the processes for later use.

Start your heirs out working in your company in departments that best match/utilize their skills and interests.

In this step, you'll get to see if the successors you have picked are serious, teachable, and ready, willing, and able to run your company for you on a small scale while you're still there.

Successful Succession Plan Step 3:

Once your successors have shown that they may be able to run your company in your absence, it's time to test your successors by **leaving** your company and seeing how well they do running it.

Start by leaving for 1-2 days at a time with phone/email access to you only in **extreme** emergencies, then leave for 1-2 days with no access to you, then lastly leave for a week, then 2 weeks, and then 3+ weeks and see how well your successors handle things.

Leaving for 3+ weeks may sound extreme, yet you **must** remember your end goal: for your business to be able to run for 3 to 6 months if you get hurt or sick, and a year or longer in your absence when you are seriously impaired or you pass away.

> **Once your successors have shown that they may be able to run your company in your absence, LEAVE and SEE how well they do running it.**

Once your successor(s) have shown they are able to run your business(es) in your absence for an extended period of time, the last step is to agree on terms (pay, the % of the company they'll receive, what their duties and other successors' duties are going to be in your absence), and write up a successor agreement for all affected family members/interested business parties to sign.

David Green, the owner of Hobby Lobby which does over $4 Billion/yr. in sales, has done a great job of preparing his heirs to run his business for decades to come. He set up a succession plan that requires each member of his family to contribute to the family business if they want to

> **David Green, the owner of Hobby Lobby set up a succession plan that requires each member of his family to contribute to the family business if they want to receive financial rewards from it.**

receive financial rewards from it. One thing his family did that is very unique is set up a stewardship trust that owns the business; this eliminates family in-fighting about their share of the business profits, and requires any family member that wants to help run the business abide by certain principles.[3] If you're very charity-minded, I encourage you to model the Green family's stewardship trust strategy.

If your heirs don't want to run your business, work with a business broker to arrange the sale or partial sale of your business.

Successful Succession Plan Step 4:

If **no one** in your family or in your business is able or willing to run your business in your absence, first I implore you to ask **why** that is. There's obviously a lack of empowerment or encouragement in your family and organization that is causing this, and you need to address it right away.

If your heirs don't want to run your business and you have a key staff person that is able to run your business in your absence, yet they don't possess the financial ability to buy your business from your estate, work with a business broker to arrange the sale or partial sale of your business at milestones you agree on (at a certain age, when you no longer want to run it, or when you're not capable of running the business any more). This will help your business thrive and continue to serve your clients for many years, and hopefully decades or centuries, to come.

Friend, tomorrow isn't promised to any of us. As such, don't delay on this: implement YOUR succession plan today!

Thinking about your death if you're young or you've avoided planning for it up to now may seem morbid, I know. Remember that King Solomon, the most successful business owner and richest man that ever lived, said you should **always** begin with the end in mind.

Following the above plan will help **your dreams live on** and preserve all the hard work you've put into your business.

Friend, tomorrow isn't promised to any of us. As such, don't delay on this: implement **your** succession plan today! When you do, you'll be able to sleep much more soundly knowing you've been diligent taking care of your business and your family planning for the future.

*FINAL NOTES on your Succession Plan:

1. Have attorneys write up and review your Succession Plan agreements for you before you sign them to ensure they comply with all the applicable local, national, and international laws, and be patient with the process. It can take up to 2-3 years to finalize a succession plan for large businesses and numbers of assets.
2. Make sure your advisors and spouse/other family members help create your succession plan (or at a bare minimum know about it), and you agree on who is to do what in your business when you no longer **can** or no longer **want** to run your business on a day to day basis.
3. Remember- the alternative to facing your mortality and having these challenging conversations

with your family about who will carry on your legacy when you're gone is untold heartache and loss for those you care about. Love them enough to avoid this fate. To drive home this point, I'll tell you a little story. A lady estate planner I know had a billionaire family client they created a robust succession plan for. They addressed all the items my friend advised them to figure out, and this **one** omission cost the family over $2 Billion when the family business patriarch passed away. Learn from this family's costly mistakes, and cover **all** the bases your advisor counsels you to address. You and your family will be glad you did.

CHAPTER 6

Keeping Your Dreams Alive - (Part 2) Systems!

In the last chapter, I spoke about the importance of creating a succession plan for your business so that it doesn't die soon after you do. Here I'm going to share a couple of other keys things you should do to make sure your dreams of making a big impact with your business don't die with you.

It comes down to this: **systems**.

If you've read the book "The E-Myth" then you know the power of systems. If you have not read it, I strongly recommend that you do! Systems are simply documented processes for how your business runs. Once they have been documented simply enough, a new employee should be able to learn them quickly, and do a good job for a client following the instructions. Systems enable your business to have rapid growth while your customers are able to consistently get good service.

If you **don't** have good systems in place, your clients will experience inconsistency in the quality of your products and services, which is **very** bad for your business long-term. Another **huge** benefit to having systems put in place in your business is that once your team is trained in following your systems, your business can run without you.

> **Once your team is trained in following your systems, your business can run without you.**

Why is this great news???

It means you can take more vacations!!! It means that your business can survive without you... even long after you're gone. This can help you sleep well at night. You will know your clients will be well taken care of both in the **near** future and in the **long-term**.

So now that we've gone over the top 2 benefits to having your business systemized (consistency of service and freedom for you!), let's go over the steps you should take to put systems in place in your business, as well as some best practices for your success.

Take these steps to systematize your business so it can run without you ASAP:

Systems can help you sleep well at night knowing your clients will be well taken care of both in the NEAR future and in the LONG-TERM.

SYSTEMIZATION STEP 1- Document your processes.

Write down the important steps you take for each of your business' main processes- for handling incoming calls, scheduling appointments, marketing, sales, HR, client interactions, etc.

> # Have team members that are the best at different tasks document how they do them.

Make sure to identify tasks that only you know how to do now, then document the steps needed to do those tasks so others can learn to do them ASAP.

NOTE: You don't have to do all the documentation of your processes. Have different team members that are the best at different tasks document how **they** do them, and if you have multiple people in different departments have them each document how they do things so everyone can learn from each other.

NOTE 2: If team members don't like to write, have them record their computer screen while they do different tasks, then have another worker write out the steps they follow watching the video.

Screen Recording Documentation Tips:

1. Keep videos to a maximum of 20-30 minutes. If documenting a long process, it's best to make multiple short screen recordings of 15-20 minutes each.

2. Have your staff talk about why they do steps the way they do them so other staff modeling them will be clear about the **what** and **why** of your systems.

3. Techsmith's Jing app will record 5 minute videos for free, and for Macs, Quicktime is great for recording your screen.

> **Have your staff talk about why they do steps the way they do them so other staff will be clear about the WHAT and WHY of your systems.**

SYSTEMIZATION STEP 2 - train staff to do tasks.

I recommend that you have weekly trainings, then delegate tasks. The book "The Ultimate Sales Machine" has many great checklists and tips for doing staff trainings.[1] I highly recommend you read it and model it. The author Chet Holmes built two different companies to over $1 Billion in sales using his 10 systems with training.

> **The book "The Ultimate Sales Machine" has many great checklists and tips for doing staff trainings, and I highly recommend you read it/model it.**

Do trainings regularly and track the results your team is generating so that your staff can duplicate 80% of your results consistently.

Anything you measure will automatically improve because attention is being paid to it.

Have **all** your staff document their work **and** the results they produce so you can see what's working and what needs to be improved. Either the system itself **or** the implementation of it may need improvement from time to time.

Is 80% efficiency not good enough to you? Never fear, my friend. The last step will raise the number dramatically!! :)

> **Have ALL your staff document their work AND the results they produce, so you can see what's working and what needs to be improved.**

SYSTEMIZATION STEP 3 - Optimize team results.

Six Sigma is a group of **very** intelligent people that discuss the best ways to do things. Fortunately for you, they created a system you can model to *now get to 99% efficiency with any system.*

Here's how you do it:

A) You document a process 80% of the way, then give the document to a key staff person that's very detail-oriented to document 80% of the remaining 20% of the process you didn't document yet.

B) Next, they or another staff person documents/optimizes 80% of the remaining 4% of the process, giving your team 99% efficiency in your processes. 80% + 16% (.8 x 20) + 3% (.8 x 4) = 99%! :)

TWO FINAL IMPORTANT NOTES on Systematizing Your Business:

Important Note #1:

A friend of mine recently shared that the only reason their business isn't 3-5 times bigger than it is today is that they are challenged in hiring quality people quickly enough. This

> # Document a process 80% of the way, then give the document to a key staff person that's very detail-oriented to document 80% of the remaining 20% of the process you didn't document yet.

challenge is costing him tens of millions of dollars, and the first step to improve something is to recognize a constraint, then improve on it.

Here's my recommendation for you to deal with constraints most powerfully:

1. Get counsel regularly on identifying and addressing challenges most powerfully, and

2. delegate tasks to address them ASAP! On tasks you're not good at, have a staff person that's best at it document the process and take over the task for you ASAP. If no one on your team is great at a task yet, model best practices from companies that produce training materials (like Zappos Insights)[2], then hire someone to do it and document their processes for you and train other team members on how to do it.

> **Get counsel regularly on identifying and addressing challenges most powerfully, and delegate tasks to address them ASAP!**

Dan Sullivan of StrategicCoach.com and Alex Charfen of Charfen.com both have excellent coaching programs to help you scale your business to the next level, and Alex has even helped billionaires grow their businesses using his systems. If getting input from advisors, coaches, and counselors is key to billionaire Elon Musk and trillionaire King Solomon's success, it's vital for you as well.

> # Dan Sullivan and Alex Charfen both have excellent coaching programs to help you scale your business to the next level.

Important Note #2:

The worst number to have of anything in business is 1. It's not only a lonely number... it's a **dangerous** #! If you only have 1 key staff that can do a task, as soon as they get sick or leave, your business will suffer. Solve this by having at least **two** of everything in your business. Work with 2 banks (Richard Branson's rule), have 2 of each key type of vendor you work with, and have at least 2 team members know how to do every key task in your business. Once you have this redundancy in place, you'll have a very stable business.

Important Note #3:

Usually in successful families, the family's home culture will be different than the business culture, and when there's a conflict between the two, the family culture wins.

Usually in successful families, the family's home culture will be different than the business culture. This is important because as family members work in the business, what will naturally happen is the family cultural norms will override your business culture when there's a conflict between the two. For example, if at home you've developed the habit of giving your children what they want when they throw a temper tantrum, you'll usually do the same thing when they're working at the office.

This will be detrimental to morale at your office if not dealt with strategically, especially if you hold other staff accountable to a higher level than you do your family members. To solve this, choose to *hold family members to the same level of account as other staff when they're at work, and seek to deal fairly with your family and hold them accountable outside of the work setting as well.* This way no resentment grows either between your family or between your staff and your family members at work.

There are **lots** of dynamics to address when it comes to managing your family members working at your company, and I highly recommend you read Quentin Fleming's book "Keep the Family Baggage Out of the Family Business"[3] for the best advanced strategies on preparing your heirs to run your business successfully for many generations to come.

Well, there you have it, friend. I recommend you put the above items in your calendar ASAP and **do them**... then you'll have a business that can run without you for very long stretches of time....and your business will truly serve **you** and your clients much better- which is its' purpose!!

CHAPTER 7

They did WHAT with your money?!?!?

Imagine you have $50 Million in the bank, your best friend's house burns down, their insurance doesn't reimburse them due to some technicality (insurance companies are good at that), and your friend doesn't have enough money to buy a new home.

What would you do? If possible you'd likely buy them a new house, or at least give them the money to pay their down payment on a new home, wouldn't you?

Say they find a typical American $200,000 home to buy, so you give them the $40,000 they need for the down payment.

Now fast forward 2 months and you run into your friend, so you catch up. "How are you enjoying your new home?" you ask. In the course of your conversation, you find out that they only bought a $100,000 house so their down payment was only $20K, and they used your other $20,000 to go on a fancy vacation!!

Often you give money to a worthy cause, and you find out a lot of the hard-earned funds you give are spent on things that don't help the cause at all.

How would you feel in this situation? Angry, upset, frustrated, shocked?! You'd likely be upset that they didn't use the money for its' intended purposes, right?!?

Well, sadly this happens with charities all the time! There are few things more satisfying than being able to share your success with others, and it's great to be able to make a difference by helping causes you care about deeply with your money or your time.

You give money to a worthy cause, and when doing research you find out that a lot of the hard-earned funds you gave are spent on things that don't help the cause at all.

As in the best friend example above, while there are many benefits to helping others, there are great risks that come with it too. A lot of your money could potentially be wasted unless you address these risks. In a little while I'll show you how to address these risks so the hard-earned money you donate actually helps those you want to help.

*Here are the biggest **risks** you face when giving money to charity:*

> **While there are many benefits to helping others, there are great risks that come with it too.**

Charitable Giving Risk #1: Wasted Funds

Most charities are very wasteful- so wasteful that less than 50% of the funds donated to them actually go to benefit their "cause." They have lots of overhead and waste funds on lavish, unnecessary expenses. In fact, many celebrity charities are so wasteful that only 15-20% of the money they raise actually goes to its' intended recipients! This is beyond sad- it's sickening really.

And it's not just celebrity charities that are wasteful; it's a large percentage of the charity industry as a whole. The book "Lords of Poverty"[1] outlines the wastefulness of many charities in great detail.

> **Most charities are so wasteful that often less than 50% of the funds donated to them actually go to benefit their "cause."**

The worst example of charity waste I read about was the story of an executive from a large charity on the way to Africa to do some studies. The executive was flying first class, and he told the person sitting next to him that the study they were doing on how to address a particular need would take 6 months and cost over $1 Million to complete.

While doing the study, the charity executive was staying in a very expensive hotel and being driven around in a Land Rover everywhere he went. Of course, he required a body guard and an interpreter!

By hiring local competent people to do the study, the charity likely could have had the study completed for $150,000 or less. It would

Chuck Feeney, has given over $9 Billion to charity work. He's given so much to Irish and Vietnamese college education that he's almost single-handedly supercharged those countries' economies.

most likely have been completed much faster. This $850,000 waste is just one example of thousands of wasteful practices by many charities.

Contrast that example to Chuck Feeney, the billionaire that gave away 90% of his wealth back in the mid-1980s.

He flies coach everywhere he goes, he keeps his charity's overhead very low, and he's given over $9 Billion to charity work in the past 30 years. He's given so much to Irish and Vietnamese college education that he's almost single-handedly supercharged those countries' economies with high-tech workers trained in the colleges he funded.[2] Now that's an amazing impact!

If you give too much money to a charity too fast, you can ruin them. How do you find charities that produce the highest ROI and impact?

Sadly, if you're giving money to a large charity, they're more likely to be wasting your money on frivolous expenses like the charity doing the $1 Million study than to be thrifty like Chuck Feeney.

Which leads me to the big question: HOW do you find charities like Chuck

Feeney's that aren't wasteful and produce the highest ROI and impact with your hard-earned charity dollars? I'll show you how to find charities that will make the **biggest** impact with the funds you give them shortly. But first, there's one more risk you must be aware of...

Charitable Giving Risk #2: More $ = SMALLER impact?

If you give too much money to a charity too fast, you can ruin them. Most chari-

> # Charities will usually produce LESS results per dollar given to them when they receive too large of a donation; in fact, the $100 Million that Mark Zuckerberg gave to the Newark, NJ school system in 2010 didn't make any meaningful impact on the students' performance.

ties are small, and if you give $2 Million to a charity that has a normal $1 Million/year operating budget ($300K overhead and $700K goes to the actual charity recipients), they'll feel pressured to "produce results" for you and often waste a lot of money attempting to spend/invest it quickly.

Due to this haste and waste, charities will usually produce **less** results per dollar given to them when they receive too large of a donation; in fact, if their overhead gets too big a large donation can even lead to the charity closing and no longer being able to serve the needy.

When YOU give to a charity, you don't want your money wasted, right?

Here are a few examples to drive home the risks of giving too large a donation to a charity:

Stories A & B: In the March 21, 2016 issue of Forbes magazine, it reveals that the $100 Million that Mark Zuckerberg gave to the Newark, NJ school system in 2010 didn't make a meaningful impact on the students' performance.

In the same issue, you learn that the $2 Billion the Gates Foundation gave to create smaller classroom sizes in America "in many of the schools we invested in, did not improve students' achievement in any significant way," according to Bill Gates himself.[3]

$2.1 Billion wasted...it's very sad, isn't it? Unfortunately results like this from big donations is common.

Story C: I know a guy named Steve that very passionately supports charities in his local area. These charities work to prevent and treat drug abuse among both teens and adults. One of the charities got a grant for an amount that was triple their normal operating budget, misused the funds, and may need to close their doors as donors are reluctant to donate more funds to them based on how they handled the grant money.

If the American Cancer Association found and promoted a cure for cancer, they would have little to do after that.

I know when you give to a charity, you don't want your money wasted, right? And you want to earn a good Return on Investment ("R.O.I." going forward) on your money, just like anything else you contribute your time and money to, right?

Here are the 4 best solutions to maximize the R.O.I. of your charitable giving and best address the charitable giving risks listed above:

Charity Solution 1: Make sure the charity doesn't have any conflicts of interests between solution they're working on and their existence. In addition to large waste, the book "Lords of Poverty" also reveals that often large charities have inherent conflicts of interest. For example, if the American Cancer Association actually found and promoted a cure for cancer, they would have little to do after that, their donations would go down significantly, and they'd have to fire a lot of their staff or may go out of business completely. Thus, they have a built-in motivation **not** to find a cure for cancer to preserve their jobs and their existence.

Charity Solution 2: Research those charities that are working in the areas in which you want to make a difference to see how efficient they are. There are many agencies that rate the efficiency of charities. Doing your own research can allow you to choose to give money to one that gives 80% or 90% of every dollar donated to the actual cause, rather than giving to a charity that only gives 50% or less of every dollar to the actual cause. Doing this research is easier than ever today. In the U.S., 501(c)3 non-profits' tax returns are public record. That means you can look up their financial records on your own. I recommend researching independent agencies' ratings of any charity you think about donating to first,[4] then ask them how big their overhead is, and *then* donate to them.

> **Personally, I only donate to groups where at LEAST 80% of every dollar goes to the actual cause.**

In my experience, when I want to donate to a cause, I've almost always been able to find a charity to donate to that has a 20% or smaller overhead.

So personally, I only donate to groups where at LEAST 80% of every dollar goes to the actual cause. I recommend you look for charities with overhead of 20% or less, as well.

It is WELL WORTH the time investment to find charities that are willing to be held accountable.

**Some of the best charities keep their overhead as low as only 10% to 12%. When you find them, work with them!

Charity Solution 3: Track results and give funds quarterly, not annually. Before giving money to a charity, I recommend you call them and find out how often they provide donors with results generated from their funds. Most only give an annual report, and I recommend you request quarterly statements showing results produced from money you've given them modeling GlimmerOfHope.org. GlimmerOfHope uses a simple 2-page Excel summary to track results produced, so it isn't overly complex for the charity to fill out.

The bigger the charity organization, the more their workers think like government beaurocrats and the less motivation they have to keep their costs low. As such, you'll likely find smaller to medium-size charities will be most willing to be held accountable by sharing the results they're generating with your funds. For this reason, you'll likely get the biggest social R.O.I. working with medium to small-size charities, and that's why I recommend you focus on working mainly with them!

You'll likely need to call several charities that work in a particular area or that address a particular need in order to find some that will give you quarterly statements and it is well worth the time investment to find charities that are willing to be held accountable.

You'll likely get the BIGGEST social R.O.I. working with medium to small-size charities.

The good news is you don't have to reinvent the wheel to do this.

I highly recommend you read the chapter of the book "Richistan" called 'Performance Philanthropy' about Philip Berber and how his charity www. GlimmerOfHope.org produce **very** large results donating to non-profits in Africa.[5]

Just one example of the kinds of breakthroughs modeling Mr. Berber's approach is this: by surveying local farmers in one village, they found that better irrigation would greatly improve their crop yield. GlimmerOfHope worked with a local non-profit and helped the farmers implement a cutting-edge irrigation system very cost-effectively, and the farmers increased their average annual income from $110/year to $1,200/year.

CCT is so efficient that within 6 months their new offices are self-sufficient with % earned from its' microloans!

Another example is the Center for Transformation ("CCT" – www.CCT.org.ph), a microfinance group in the Philippines that does over 150,000 microloans/year. CCT keeps their overhead under 15%; they're so efficient that when they open an office in a new town, within 6 months the office is self- sufficient with the interest earned from its' microloans!

Donating quarterly protects your money from being wasted and gives you more excitement about the difference you're making.

They also help their partners with banking, housing, and funding their children's schooling.

Once you're holding the charity groups accountable by tracking the results they're producing quarterly, the next step to maximize your social R.O.I. is to give them donations in smaller amounts quarterly.

Say a charity you support wants to expand an existing program by $100,000 this year; you agree to fund the program expansion. Instead of writing them a $100,000 check, give them $25,000 for the first quarter, and measure what the money produces after the first quarter. If it's producing results, you give the next $25,000 for the 2nd quarter. Give them another $25,000 for the 3rd quarter, and the last $25,000 for the 4th quarter. This strategy will benefit both you and the charity you're supporting. For you, it will protect your money from being

> **In addition to giving money accountably on an ongoing basis, consider donating time and expertise to charities.**

wasted and give you more excitement about the difference you're making as you're monitoring your donation's results more closely. For the charity, it helps them think more like businesspeople and improve their performance. It causes them to use your monies wisely.

Charity Solution 4: In addition to giving accountability on an ongoing basis, consider donating time and expertise to charities you work with, to help them improve. This may seem like a big commitment, but often you can help them immensely even if you have only a small amount of time to donate.

If you are retired, you can volunteer 20 hours a week to charities. If the charity is local, you can volunteer in person. If they're in a different country than you, you can still serve them virtually on a board of advisors or as a consultant. For example, I know one micro-finance charity in the Philippines that has business owners from several different countries who give free consulting by the hour to the charity's clients on Skype. Even if you're a busy business owner or executive working lots of hours, you can donate as little as 1-2 hours per month serving on a charity's

> # No matter how busy you are, there is a way to donate time to charities. Reach out to them, and see what they need help with most!

board of advisors and attending monthly meetings via phone or Skype.

No matter how busy you are or how much free time you have, there is a way to donate time to charities you care about. Think creatively, reach out to them, and see what they need help with! You may find that your expertise helps them just as much as or **more** than the money you donate to them helps them. And you'll be very fulfilled knowing your expertise is helping them. It's a win-win - a win for the charity, the people they serve, and you. :)

> **Work on building a legacy that lasts beyond your lifetime. It's the most important work you'll ever do.**

In closing, on the topic of maximizing your impact through giving to others, I want to challenge you to think creatively and test conventional wisdom about two key ideas:

First, "giving back" is whack. It's very common to hear wealthy people saying how committed they are to giving back, and the media often uses this phrase.

I say the phrase needs to be replaced ASAP! "Giving back" infers that what you have was given to you, which cannot be further from the truth. You earned the wealth you have, often at great sacrifice to you and your family. If you choose to give to others, wonderful! Yet please refer to your kindness accurately as social investing, and gently correct those that wrongly say you're giving back. This way you don't empower those that want to demonize you for your success and create class warfare in society, and you'll still inspire others to be generous as well.

Second, be creative with the metrics you use to measure the impact of your giving. Recently, Larry Page said he'd rather leave his wealth to Elon Musk than charities, because he thought Elon could make a bigger positive impact on the world than charities could.[6] Richard Branson said that business itself can be a force for good, so don't think the only way you can help those less fortunate is to give to charities. Look to maximize the positive impact you make on society through charities **and** your business, and consider joining forces with other like-minded successful families to crowdsource bigger projects. Several billionaires are doing this through their family offices, and I think it's a great strategy to use the MasterMind principle powerfully. King Solomon himself built his $1.5+ Trillion fortune MasterMinding at the highest level ever seen, so model him and current billionaires by teaming up with other powerful people to do great things!

Well, that about sums up this strategy. *I encourage you to commit to* **now** *avoiding your charity dollars being wasted, and to earning the maximum social R.O.I. from every charity dollar you donate going forward.* When you do this, you'll make the biggest impact with maximum joy for the rest of your life... and possibly even beyond! (More on that in the next chapter... especially how you can keep your family involved for many generations to come.)

My friend, continue to work on building a legacy that lasts. It's the most important work you'll ever do.

CHAPTER 8

How to get what you CAN'T buy...

In the last 7 chapters, I've showed you how to ensure your business serves your clients and your family after you're gone, how to empower your family for generations by **now** passing on your inheritance to them, and how to make the biggest impact possible working effectively with charities.

The summary of all these strategies: maximize your fulfillment, your impact, and your legacy.

*So, how **can** you get what you can't buy? Am I talking about love? Eternal youth? Living forever? It's actually a little of all 3, and I'll reveal that to you in a moment...*

The Beatles' song famous line, "You can't buy me love," is true. It's **also** true that you can't buy lasting fame or respect, or the holy grail fountain of youth to live forever.

However, you can be remembered and still be making a significant impact many generations after you're gone with the right strategies. You can do this if you're a billionaire like Richard Branson, Bill Gates, Warren Buffet, or other Giving Pledge members today, and even if you aren't.

> # You can be remembered and still making a significant impact many generations after you're gone with the right strategies.

Andrew Carnegie is a great example of leaving a lasting impact. He gave all his money to charity by the time he died, and he funded Carnegie Hall in New York, Carnegie Mellon University in Pittsburgh, and hundreds of public libraries across the U.S.A. Even though most Americans today don't know much about him except that he was in the steel industry, his impact is felt every time someone fills their mind with new knowledge at one of the libraries he built.

Andrew Carnegie decided to give all his money to charity while still alive and die broke. Others give all their wealth to their family when they die, and their heirs squander it quickly. *Other successful people like you set up foundations that support charities for multiple generations after they're gone* (like the Ford Foundation that Henry Ford started) and trusts to empower their family long-term.

Balance leaving an inheritance for your family and giving money to charity, so you can make the biggest impact on the world with your life.

How do you decide which strategy is best for YOUR family?

From all my research of successful families, I've discovered that *the best strategy is to balance leaving an inheritance for your family and giving money to charity* **so you can make the biggest total** *impact on the world* with your life. The satisfaction from making a big, lasting difference can't be bought... yet it can be gained with the right strategies!

*Let's review the biggest challenges standing in your way of leaving a **long**-lasting legacy so you can address them most powerfully...*

Legacy Challenge 1: Giving heirs too much wealth.

How can you avoid ruining your children so they don't up like Paris Hilton or Kim Kardashian?

You've likely heard the horror stories of wealthy heiresses like Paris Hilton or Kim Kardashian embarrassing their families. Both of those "lady's" fame started with home-made porn!! In fact, Paris Hilton embarrassed her grandfather so much that he took her out of the family will. What went wrong? How can you avoid ruining your children so they don't end up like a Paris Hilton or Kim Kardashian?

Many wealthy parents wring their hands struggling with how much money to leave their children so those children don't have to struggle in life, yet they aren't made lazy and ruined by the wealth they receive. In fact, billionaire Giving Pledge members discuss this challenge very often with each other. How much money is enough? How much money is too much to leave them? These are good questions to ask, but there are even better ones you and your spouse should be asking.

One way to address this risk is to put perfor-mance clauses in trusts you set up for your heirs so they have to behave cer-tain ways to receive their funds. That is what 99% of estate planners you speak with would tell you to do to keep your children from embarrassing your family.

How much money is enough? And how much money is too much to leave your heirs?

These trusts are only minimally successful in "keep-ing children in line," and they usually strain your rela-tionship with each other because they don't address the root causes of unhealthy behavior.

The challenge is more than just the amount of money your heirs are given. The root problem is a lack of training and a modeling of the best eti-quette, morals, and values; the true problem is the condition of your heirs' hearts. In a moment, I'll show you the best way to address the root heart challenges for your heirs.

Legacy Challenge 2: Creating bitterness in your heirs

The ROOT problem is lack of training and modeling of the best etiquette, morals, and values-basically, the condition of your heirs' hearts.

If you leave your heirs lots of money because of your love for them, then why do they often end up bitter towards you? This perplexes most wealthy parents like you, and it's very frustrating. For most wealthy heirs, the anger and bitterness stem from not being empowered enough to manage what they were left, and from not having their worth validated.

In many families, talking about money is taboo, so parents create estate plans for leaving money to their heirs and charities without **ever** discussing it with their family. This usually leads to many negative reactions in family members when parents die, as the first time they're hearing about their parents' wishes is in an ultra-emotional state of grief. Avoid this at all costs!! If you don't, you're running a 90%+ risk of leading your family towards Financial Success Failure as I wrote about a few chapters back. This combined with lack of preparation to handle your wealth is a recipe for disaster.

The **good news** is there's a simple, yet powerful solution to this challenge while I'll reveal to you in just a moment.

Legacy Challenge 3: Unclear long-term charity strategies

> **For most wealthy heirs, the anger and bitterness stem from not being empowered enough to manage what you leave them and from not validating their worth.**

As I mentioned above, Andrew Carnegie gave away virtually all his wealth to charity during his lifetime. Other families like the Fords set up foundations that give away a smaller percentage of their funds (a.k.a. their "endowment") yearly so that they live on for multiple generations.

At first glance, one of the 2 models may seem like the best fit for you, and they each have specific challenges that must be addressed. Here are just a few examples:

> **Andrew Carnegie gave away virtually all his wealth to charity during his lifetime. Other families set up foundations that live on for multiple generations.**

If you set up a Carnegie-style 'spend down' foundation that still has a significant amount of wealth in it when you die, how do you ensure your heirs finish what you started and put the funds towards the causes you want them to go to? How do you avoid your heirs suing your estate and fighting over the funds?

If you set up a perpetual foundation like

the Ford Foundation, how do you ensure the funding goes to charities that you'd approve of decades after you're gone? How do you avoid the funding going to causes that you'd **never** support if you were alive?

For example, if you're a die-hard libertarian that believes in 100% personal responsibility and limited government, you'd turn over in your grave if your foundation was giving funds to expand the welfare state in your country, right? How do you ensure this doesn't happen?

How do you avoid your heirs suing your estate and fighting over the funds?

These are the main challenges you need to address if you want to leave a positive, powerful legacy that lasts for multiple generations.

*Without further ado, let's get right to those Long-Term Legacy Solutions **now**, shall we friend!!*

Long-Term Legacy Solution #1:
EMPOWER Your Heirs with True Wealth

> # It's vital you address the challenges of how much wealth to leave your heirs so they are empowered and not made lazy or embarrassments to your family

As I stated earlier, it's vital you address the challenges of how much wealth to leave your heirs so they are empowered and not made lazy or embarrassments to your family, and to address the root causes of squandering your wealth through training and modeling the best skillsets, morals, and values to your heirs.

Here are the 3 steps I recommend you take ASAP to empower your heirs with true lasting wealth:

Step A: Commit to yearly passing on your inheritance to your family so they are NOW

empowered to manage what you've built once you're gone.

The best way to do this is the following:

i) Host your Family Vault Meetings every year so that your skillsets, morals, and values are passed on to all family members yearly, and at each FVM make decisions as a family with your Family Counsel. This way you both learn from each others' experiences **and** actively make decisions together as a family. This will help ensure everyone in your family is actively involved in building and strengthening your family. :)

ii) Invite your heirs to do small things in your family business at first, then invite them to do more and more things as their interest and skills grow; look

> **Yearly pass on your inheritance to your family so they are NOW empowered to manage what you've built once you're gone.**

to give them tasks to do that utilize their strengths, and through this process, you may create the desire in one or more of your heirs to manage your family business. To avoid entitlement in your children ["Pride comes before a fall,"[1] King Solomon warns us], regularly remind them that your family success was earned with skill development and focused work, and make them work in your business to earn positions of management. This way they'll manage your business much better long-term.

iii) Do charity work together every year. Do this by deciding what charities to support and reviewing the results your charitable work produced in the past year in your Family Counsel meetings, **and** by volunteering your time to charities as a family and discussing what the experience was like for each family member.

> **Invite your heirs to do small things in your family biz; look to give them tasks to do that utilize their strengths.**

Step B: Seek wisdom from advisors on how much money to leave to your family and how much money to leave to charity.

King Solomon said that a wise man leaves an inheritance to his children's children,[2] and as we discussed earlier, hosting your Family Vault Meetings yearly is the best way to empower your heirs with their true inheritance of your skills, knowledge, and values. Once your next FVM is scheduled, the next step is to decide how much financial wealth to leave to charity and how much to leave to your heirs. Leaving all your money to charity is unkind to your heirs, and leaving all your money to your heirs is unkind also, as it may very well tempt them to be lazy. As such, it's wisest to give a portion of your financial wealth to both charity and to your heirs.

> **Decide how much financial wealth to leave to charity, and how much to leave to your heirs.**

There is no hard and fast rule on how much money to give your heirs. As such, you need great discernment in making these decisions. Based on my study of many successful families, I recommend you follow this system for leaving money to your heirs:

Whether in their allowance or income, a trust you've set up for them, or in a loan your Family Vault gave them to start a business, start by leaving them small amounts at first and larger amounts later.

The ancient maxim "he who is faithful with little will be faithful with much"[3] applies here; hold the funds accountable, and make it clear that your accountability is to empower your heirs to wisely manage funds so they are successful in life, **not** to control them.

Leave your heirs small amounts at first and larger amounts later.

I highly recommend you share how you're managing the family wealth with your heirs during your FVMs as well (share details on an age-appropriate basis depending on how involved family members are in your family business). Demonstrating trust, humility, and leadership in this way will help to build strong trust in your family.

Step C: Measure how well your heirs are managing wealth you've left them already.

As soon as your heirs can add/subtract/multiply at 6 or 7 years old, have them follow the Rockefeller rules[4]: give 10% of your income to charity, save 10%, then track what you do with the other 80%. **All** results improve with measurement and accountability, so the more of this you do as a family, the better!

> **Follow the Rockefeller rules: give 10% of your income to charity, save 10%, then track what you do with the other 80%.**

Long-Term Legacy Solution #2: Avoid/Heal Family Bitterness

This is some of the hardest work you'll do as a family to leave a powerful legacy, and it's also some of the most important work you'll do as a family as well. Why?

You're likely very successful already and now committed to maximum success for yourself and your family moving forward. Like most driven, successful people, you are great at focusing on your work. A big challenge most successful people like you face is that it's easy to be so engulfed in your work that you neglect to spend enough time with your family, which often leads to disempowerment and bitterness.

What are the best ways to address these 2 challenges of disempowerment and bitterness?

a) *Do charity work together as a family.* This not only is a bonding experience for your family; it also has many extra benefits as well! It grows responsibility, empathy for those less fortunate, grants another perspective to life, and may cause gratitude in the hearts of your heirs. Now those are some great side effects, aren't they?! It may open up a door of

> **Most successful people like you neglect to spend enough time with your family, which often leads to disempowerment and bitterness.**

opportunity for you or your children to develop deeper compassion and kindness, which may spill over into your relationships to one another.

b) Affirm your family members for who they are, not just what they do. As a parent, it's easy to only affirm our children for good behavior. And as you're a high performer, your children likely feel great pressure to live up to your and others' expectations to be like you.

The combination of these 2 factors likely has driven your children to either work their butt off to win your approval, or to give up on trying to impress you. Whether they've worked hard to win your approval or not, either way your children have likely wondered if they are "good enough" for you. To address this challenge most powerfully, affirming them for

What are the best ways to address these 2 challenges? Do charity work together as a family, and affirm your family members for who they are.

who they are will help heal past wounds of rejection so your heirs will carry on your legacy with maximum power, contentment, joy, love, and impact.

> **Whether they've worked hard to win your approval or not, either way your children have likely wondered if they are good enough for you.**

How do you do this? Begin by writing down what you appreciate about each member of your family. Write down their strengths and skills- the positive things that make them unique that you appreciate.

Next, as soon as possible tell them that you love them for who they are, you're glad they're in your life, and tell them some of the things you appreciate about them. Ideally tell them this in person or at the least on video chat or on the phone.

Don't send them this message via text or email; let them hear your emotion so that your validation really touches their heart.

Most of our culture is performance-based, so your validation of your heirs as an important part of your family will mean a lot to them. Lastly, affirm your spouse and children regularly using the strategies outlined in chapter 3 of this book. In Jewish culture, parents verbally bless and affirm their children weekly, and Jewish people make up 30% of the Forbes 400 list. Coincidence? I think not. Your tongue has the power to give life and to destroy; choose to speak life into your family, and watch them flourish!

> ## Most of our culture is performance-based, so your validation of your heirs as an important part of your family will mean a lot to them.

c) *Invest time with your family members regularly to validate their importance to you.* You don't have to invest hours and hours per day with your family or become "SuperDad" to be a good parent. Actually, a few hours where you're present and engaged with them is better than being home with your family 10 hours/week and on your smartphone the whole time. It's good to invest family time as a whole **and** 1 on 1 with different family members. Jim Sheil's book "The Family Board Meeting" has some great strategies to connect with your children at a deeper level in a quarterly, 1 on 1 meeting with them individually... even if they're distant teenagers. I highly recommend you read his book, and do quarterly 1 on 1 meetings with each of your children, in addition to your Family Vault Meetings. I've been doing them with my sons, and they've been great at opening up important conversations.

Connect with your children at a deeper level in a quarterly, 1 on 1 meeting with them individually...

Lastly, do not ignore real issues. If there have been problems in the past with your relationship, admit it. If some of the problem has been you, confess that you have been less than what you had wanted to be. If the problem is with them, be gently confrontational. When we really love someone, we do not allow problems to go unaddressed. Sweeping things under the rug does not make them go away. It merely gives us something to stumble over in the future! Care enough to be honest with your spouse, your children and yourself!

Long-Term Legacy Solution #3: Clear Charity Objectives

With your family charity strategy, it's vital that you are very clear on your objectives. The first thing you should decide is whether to set up a spend-down foundation or a perpetual one.

> # With your family charity, decide whether to set up a spend-down foundation or a perpetual one.

Spend-down foundation:

PROS- you have a say in how your charity funds are invested while you're alive, and you get the satisfaction of seeing greater results from your giving **as long as** you hold the charities you donate to accountable.

CONS: your donations stop after you're gone, limiting your ability to empower charities long -term. As such, going this route make sure you set a target age/date for all your money to be spent (I recommend age 85).

Perpetual foundation:

PROS- you can support charities for multiple generations, creating a continuity of relationships. CONS: your family must manage investments that produce cashflow to give to charities; as such, it's a much bigger commitment.

> # With a perpetual foundation, you can support charities for multiple generations, creating a continuity of relationships.

Seeing if your heirs want to manage your business after you're gone or if they want to run their own businesses, can help you determine if a spend-down or perpetual foundation makes the most sense for your family. Also, if your children are passionate about supporting the same type charities as you, a perpetual foundation may make more sense for you. Discuss all these factors, then decide what's best for you and your family.

The second objective to clarify is how to operate your foundation. Whether it's a spend-down or perpetual one, be clear on your qualifications for managers, what are the qualifications for the charities you give to, and how to communicate with and hold charities accountable on an on-going basis. I recommend you put these details in your foundation's by-laws so they're followed, especially with a perpetual foundation.

Lastly, determine how you'll work with charities. I recommend you make submitting 2-page quarterly accountability reports a requirement for charities you work with in your founda-

> **If your children are passionate about supporting the same type charities as you, a perpetual foundation may make more sense for you.**

tion's by-laws. Reinforce this to your family in Family Vault meetings as well. Have your whole family review the results of your giving every year, so even young children get in the habit of directing resources towards endeavors that are producing a good return, and learn how to measure charity's resulting social ROI.

> **By involving your family in your charity work, you'll empower them with youthful energy, excitement, and hope for the future.**

Well, there you have it, friend. When you follow the formula above, you'll leave a powerful, lasting legacy.

You can't buy love, but you'll empower your family with deeper love for each other and their fellow man. You can't buy eternal youth, but by involving your family in your charitable work you'll empower them with youthful energy, excitement, and hope for the future as you see yourselves make a positive difference in the world.

You can't buy eternal life, but by investing your life strategically and leaving wealth to both your heirs and charities, you'll enrich the world, be thought of fondly, and be making a positive impact on others through your family 30, 50, and perhaps even 100 or 300 years after you're gone.

Now **that's** a legacy to get excited about leaving, isn't it!!!

> **Leaving wealth to both your heirs and charities, you'll enrich the world, be thought of fondly, and be making a positive impact on others through your family 30, 50, perhaps even 100 or 300 years after you're gone.**

CONCLUSION

I congratulate you for wisely investing your time in reading this book. To maximize your R.O.I. from your investment, **now** do the following things:

1. Review your written notes from reading this book, and create a written action plan to implement to maximize your family legacy- define manhood, affirm your heirs, plan your next Family Vault Meeting, and create a powerful Lasting Legacy Plan for your business and charitable endeavors.
2. Go over your action plan with your spouse and schedule dates to implement your family's Lasting Legacy plan.
3. To maximize your results implementing your newly improved family legacy plan, contact my office to request a LegacyBuilders consultation. We offer a variety of coaching and consulting ser-

vices to help successful families like yours ensure they **don't** throw away everything they've worked so hard to achieve, and we'll be glad to help you maximize your family legacy ASAP. During our consultation together, we'll determine which of our programs, if any, are the best fit for you and your family's specific objectives- whether attending one of our retreats, getting group or 1-on-1 coaching support, or having us help you arrange an heir Affirmation Ceremony or hosted Family Vault Meeting. Go now to <u>www.BeyondBillions.com/consult</u> to arrange your consultation.

4. If you're a billionaire, we invite you to contact our office to request information about our exclusive Solomon Wisdom Society MasterMind group. Membership is capped at 40 members (limited to only the top 2% of billionaires worldwide), and as you would expect, potential members are vetted fully before being allowed to apply to join. Call or text/WhatsApp us at +1.248.325.8872 or email us 'SWS Membership Inquiry' to <u>SWSsupport@BeyondBillions.com</u> with your name, best mailing address, and best direct phone number, and we'll send you information about SWS membership. All inquiries are kept 100% confidential.

May God richly bless you and your family for many generations to come as you now use these powerful legacy tools! *—David Roy Newby*

Wala na, kaibigan!
!Es todo, amigo!
(That's all, friend!)

Well, THAT'S ALMOST IT...

Following is a Resource Section containing several of the references I made throughout this book and financial tools for your benefit. Enjoy and put them to use.

RESOURCES

To Optimize The Way You Think:

Think and Grow Rich by Dr. Napoleon Hill (Get your FREE copies of this classic at <u>www.BeyondBillions.com/Bonuses</u>)

Psycho-Cybernetics by Dr. Maxwell Maltz (www.Psycho-Cybernetics.com)

To Live a Balanced Life in Every Way:

Passion, Profit, and Power by Marshall Sylver (www.DavidNewbyRecommends.com/sylver)

Charities That "Teach a Man How To Fish" & Charity Research Tools

By giving to charity, you set in motion the law of reciprocity: What you give out will always come back to you multiplied. Please choose charities that match your values. Below are my favorites.

Center for Community Transformation
  (www.CCT.org.ph)

They give micro business loans to poor people in the Philippines to help them start their own small businesses. These are people that banks won't allow to borrow because they "don't qualify," yet CCT has a 98 percent repayment rate for all loans! CCT also offers loans for affordable housing plus scholarships for poor students. A charity that is truly empowering people! Please learn more at their website

EndPoverty.org (www.EndPoverty.org)

Founded by Dr. James Dobson, Focus does radio broadcasts in over 100 countries to strengthen families. This charity helps bring families closer together when many forces are weakening families.

Charity Navigator (www.CharityNavigator.org)

Use this website to find out what percentage of your donations go the actual cause you want to support when giving to a nonprofit, what they spend their overhead on, and how transparent they are.

Advisors, Tools, and Resources to Help You with Succession Planning, Estate Planning, and Hosting Family Vault Meetings

Please go to www.DavidNewbyRecommends.com to get recommendations to the best resources to help you maximize your results in these areas.

REFERENCES

Introduction: Why You Want This Book

1. "UBS Global Family Office Report," Financial Times (September 2017). Website: https://www.ft.com/content/9916d776-96ff-11e7-a652-cde3f882dd7b

Chapter 1: Avoid Financial Success Failure. Say What?!?

1. Proverbs 27:6, *The Holy Bible*, New International Version (Biblica, Inc, 2011). http://www.bible-gateway.com/versions/New-International-Version-NIV-Bible. *Unless noted otherwise, all Torah/Bible scriptures quoted in "Beyond Billions" are in NIV.

2. Proverbs 13:22, *The Holy Bible*
3. The Giving Pledge- a group of billionaires that have pledged to give at least half of their wealth to charity. https://GivingPledge.org
4. 1 Kings Chapter 10, *The Holy Bible*. This chapter highlights many of Solomon's business ventures, as well as how other leaders of his day paid him hundreds of millions of dollars annually in gifts in exchange for his wise counsel.
5. Ecclesiastes 1:14, *The Holy Bible*. Ecclesiastes was written by King Solomon in his old age as he reflected on his life and accomplishments.

Chapter 2: For MANLY Men Only

1. Garrett J. White, *The Black Book: A Modern Man's Doctrine to Having It All,* (Austin, TX: Next Century Publishing, 2017): p. 20-30.
2. Proverbs 18:12, *The Holy Bible*
3. Proverbs 27:6, *The Holy Bible*
4. Proverbs 14:12, *The Holy Bible*
5. "Pornography Survey," Proven Men. Website: https://www.provenmen.org/pornography-survey-statistics-2014/
6. Ashley Vance, *Elon Musk*, (New York, NY: HarperCollins Publishers, 2015)

Chapter 3: You're my BOY, Blue!

1. Jim Sheils, *The Family Board Meeting*, (Ponte Vedra Beach, FL: Board Meeting Books, 2015): p. 36-59
2. Craig Hill, *The Power of a Parent's Blessing*, (Lake Mary, FL: Charisma House, 2013): p. 45-48

Chapter 4: Is Your Family's Success Built to Last?

1. Proverbs 29:18, *The Holy Bible* (KJV)
2. Proverbs 13:22, *The Holy Bible* (NASB)

Chapter 5: Will your dreams DIE with you or not?

1. "Inside U-Haul's Roller Coaster Ride From Nastiest Family Feud to Market Dominance," Forbes (February 2016), Website: https://www.forbes.com/sites/luisakroll/2016/02/10/inside-u-hauls-rollercoaster-ride-from-nastiest-family-feud-to-market-dominance
2. Get DISC profile tests FREE at https://www.tonyrobbins.com/disc; Kolbe tests are at http://www.kolbe.com/

3. "How to Avoid Family Fights About Your Multi-Billion Dollar Business," Wisdom to Wealth podcast. Website: http://ultimatewealthtv.tumblr.com/AvoidFamilyBusinessFights

Chapter 6: Keeping Your Dreams Alive (Part 2)- Systems!

1. Chet Holmes, *The Ultimate Sales Machine,* (New York, NY: Portfolio, 2007).
2. Zappos Insights- sharing the Zappos Culture with the World (Zappos has been voted one of the 100 best companies to work for several times). Website: www.ZapposInsights.com
3. Quentin J. Fleming, *Keep The Family Baggage Out of the Family Business: Avoiding The Seven Deadly Sins That Destroy Family Businesses,* (New York, NY: Fireside, 2000).

Chapter 7: They did WHAT with your money?!?!?

1. Graham Hancock, *Lords of Poverty: The Power, Prestige, and Corruption of the International Aid Business,* (New York, NY: Atlantic Monthly Press, 1989).

2. Conor O'Clery, *The Billionaire Who Wasn't: How Chuck Feeney Secretly Made and Gave Away A Fortune,* (New York, NY: Public Affairs, 2007).

3. "Well-Intentioned Whiffs," *Forbes* (March 21, 2016), p. 48.

4. Use https://www.charitynavigator.org/ to find out how efficient a charity you're considering donating to is with donors' funds.

5. Robert Frank, *Richistan: A Journey Through the American Wealth Boom and the Lives of the New Rich,* (New York, NY: Crown Publishers, 2007). p. 172-179.

6. "Why It Makes Sense for Larry Page to Donate His Billions to Elon Musk," Reuters (March 2014). Website: http://blogs.reuters.com/felix-salmon/2014/03/25/why-it-makes-sense-for-larry-page-to-donate-his-billions-to-elon-musk/

Chapter 8: How to get what you CAN'T buy...

1. Proverbs 16:18, *The Holy Bible*
2. Proverbs 13:22, *The Holy Bible*
3. Luke 16:10, *The Holy Bible*
4. "The Rockefeller Rules," Concentus Wealth Advisors (March 2013: p.1). Website: http://concentuswealth.com/wp-content/uploads/Valuables-vol6-Rockefeller-Rules.pdf

INDEX

BONUS GIFTS FROM DAVID ROY NEWBY

As my way of saying thanks for buying this book, I'm pleased to give you 4 bonuses worth over $821.00. But there's a small catch. All I ask is that you tell your friends about my book and invite them to invest in it, too. My wife and sons appreciate it.

Here's the 4 FREE Bonuses You'll Receive:

1. ***"Beyond Billions" BONUS Chapter.*** Learn how to model King Solomon's process for picking joint venture partners that made him a trillionaire worth as much as the richest 400 Americans combined. ($19.95 value)

2. **Family Vault Meeting planner.** Use this to plan and experience powerful annual retreats with your family in a simple, easy to learn format. ($297 value)

3. ***Solomon Says* app beta tester access.** This app is like having your favorite 10 billionaires on speed dial to ask questions when you need the best answer... only better as Solomon was the best business person ever. ($4.95 value)

4. **LegacyBuilders Consultation Credit.** Once you read this book, if you're one of the 5 percent

of people who actually use your new knowledge to improve your life, you'll want to take the next step. This entitles you to a $500 credit towards a LegacyBuilders consultation, where we'll help you build your BEST legacy possible. ($500+ value)

To claim your bonuses, NOW go to this site:
http://www.BeyondBillions.com/Bonuses.html